Rory Conde, Serial Killer

Pete Dove

Published by Trellis Publishing, 2021.

RORY CONDE, SERIAL KILLER

First edition. July 2, 2021.

Copyright © 2021 Pete Dove.

ISBN: 979-8224711321

Written by Pete Dove.

RORY CONDE, SERIAL KILLER

PETE DOVE

<u>JUANA BARRAZA</u>
<u>PETER SUTCLIFFE</u>

The killer who advised his victims

Driving from Tampa down to Miami is a popular past time for holiday makers looking to make the most out of their visit to Florida. Of course, no trip to the Sunshine State is really complete without an experience of the Everglades, and perhaps the most scenic way to do that by car is to get onto Highway 41 and enjoy the Tamiami Trail.

It's a long and well established route. One which can trace its roots back to early days of the twentieth century. But while the Trail might have represented an astonishing feat of engineering for its day little consideration was given to its impact on the Everglades themselves. Cutting West to East across the width of the Florida peninsula, the road (and a nearby canal) reduced the water flow to the natural wonder that is the Everglades, placing a severe threat not only on its own existence, but to the diverse animal and plant life that flourishes there.

Fortunately, common sense appears, after more than a century, to be raising its head. Plans are afoot to lift the road above ground, allowing a natural flow of life-giving water to chunter south towards the mangrove enhanced coastlands.

It has to be admitted that the highway loses its scenic delights as it is about to enter Miami. It is here that the road swaps views of luscious countryside for the less pleasant vista of cheap motels, strip bars and porn shops. It is this part of the cross peninsular route that will, unfortunately, feature most in our unfolding story.

There is more disappointing news. Sadly, though it remains an attractive route for the most part, the Tamiami Trail is famous as the site of another kind of carnage to the inadvertent one carried out on the Everglades. One that cannot be repealed through modern technology and environmental awareness. Because the scenic splendour of the roadway was to become the dumping ground of another Tamiami. The Tamiami Strangler. The name given to Rory Conde, who for just under a year reigned terror upon the people of South Florida in the mid-1990s.

Rory Enrique Conde was born in the swinging sixties. June 14th, 1965 to be precise. But he was not to enjoy those days of growing freedom and awareness so tainted by the horrors of Vietnam. Events which faced the population of the US back in the days when the Beatles ruled supreme, and Elvis was beginning to abandon his rock career for a life in the movies.

Because Conde was not a US citizen. Instead, he was born in Barranquilla, the largest city on the Caribbean coast of Columbia. It is an interesting place, steeped in history. The site of the city is thought to date back to the middle ages, and for a long time was regarded as the cultural capital of its country. By the late 1940s this modern city was home to a mixed bag of natives and immigrants, many those who had left Europe during the two world wars. It bore the name 'Columbia's Golden Gate' and the somewhat self-aggrandizing motto 'Barranquilla – capital of life'.

But by the time of Conde's birth the city was in decline. It was about to lose its status as Columbia's primary port, and huge and uncontrollable corruption meant that state money was directed elsewhere and into less greedy pockets. In fact, the city plunged into a seemingly terminal decline through the sixties, seventies, eighties and into the early part of the nineties.

It was into the beginning of this decline that Rory Conde joined the other half a million then inhabitants of the city. It was by now turning into a dangerous place to grow up. And, for Rory, the precarious path to adulthood was something he would face without the love of a mother. Or, at least, a love he could recall. Some dispute seems to exist regarding exactly what happened to Conde's mother. That she died of tetanus is not in question, but it appears that this happened when he was just six months old, although some reports claim he was six years of age. Whichever, he was a very young child when he and his elder sister Nelly moved to live with their paternal grandparents. Dad was out of the picture, having emigrated to Miami. But when Rory was twelve - a highly impressionable age – he went to live with his father, Gustavo. That tough childhood rapidly became much harder still.

Again, absolute clarity does not exist over what happened in Miami. That Gustavo and Rory did not get on is not in doubt. We cannot be sure why, maybe the cultural change was too great for the child, maybe Gustavo did not want his life in the states impacted by his children. It seems as though there was much emotional abuse in the household, but perhaps worse.

It is believed in some quarters that Rory was subjected to sexual abuse at the hands of his father. Indeed, Conde's spouse, Carla, remains firmly of the opinion that her former husband's violent outbursts can be traced back to that abuse he received at the hands of the person charged with his care. But even this story maybe a misinterpretation of the facts. At one of his trials (he was tried separately for one of the murders he committed) it was claimed by his lawyers that in fact it was not his father who was the abuser, but an uncle, and that this abuse happened whilst he was living with his grandparents in Columbia, taking place when he was between the ages of six and twelve.

But even this evidence is far from conclusive. Other reports place the abuse at a much earlier age, before he was two years old and cite two uncles as the culprits.

'In a very real sense, he was put on a track when he was abused as a child that was impossible for him to turn away from anymore,' claimed that attorney, Jeffrey Fink, at the trial – to which we will return later.

Carla was just fifteen years old when she married Conde. (They had met when she was only thirteen, still very much a child). That marriage took place in 1987, when he was twenty-one. Quite how such a union with one so young could be entertained is another unanswered question in the depraved matters of the future killer's life. The couple went on to have two children of their own, but their relationship was torrid. Conde was a violent husband, one whose aggressiveness towards his wife was enough to see him handed a prison sentence. The

Columbian displayed little faith towards his wife, and frequently brought home other women. By 1992, Carla had had enough, and challenged Conde over his philandering behaviour. It is hard to have anything but total sympathy for her plight. On this occasion, she had discovered a video tape her husband had made of a prostitute lying on their marital bed, wearing Carla's lingerie, and masturbating. Her husband responded violently to her challenge, assaulting Carla and earning that prison sentence.

However, she stuck by her man and after his release the two of them moved to a condo situated near to the Tamiami Trail. Again, though, the relationship struggled. The violence within the man continued to burst out. Not only did he kick and punch his younger wife, but on more than one occasion dragged her so violently across the room that she acquired carpet burns on her body. He also displayed OCD type behaviour, turning violent if he found any crumbs dropped on the floor by their baby.

It was after the spell in prison that his behaviour changed. Rory would now often be out all night, and marital relations between the two apparently ceased. He would claim defensively that he was out fishing, but never returned home with the characteristic smell of fish on his body or clothes. Further, these must have been particularly vicious and ingenious prey that he hunted, because Carla would frequently see scratch marks on his back following these 'angling sessions'. She confronted her husband about them, and that too earned her a beating.

During this time Conde's behaviour became increasingly worrying and anti-social. On one occasion Carla discovered him masturbating outside a neighbor's window. If she had friends over, he would get onto all fours and follow them if they needed the bathroom, peeking through the keyhole as they undertook their toilet. In the end, in 1994, Carla took her children away from their violent father and moved in with her own parents. Conde was determined to have the final word, threatening to kill Carla should she dare to engage in a relationship with another man.

Dual standards seemed to be something under which the violent husband operated; whether he held the moral compass to see anything wrong in this is yet another question to which there is no apparent answer.

Carla moved out of the family (if that is not too strong a word) home in the July of 1994; within two months Conde had committed his first murder. As with so much else in this unfortunate story, the event was bizarre in the extreme. Later, after he was caught and was facing questioning, Conde would maintain that it was the split from his wife which pushed him over the edge and into the world of homicide. Clearly, he was (and probably still is) a very disturbed person whose tormented upbringing must surely have played some role in his future offending. Splitting from his wife and losing his children – there is no evidence that he was ever violent towards them – must surely have pushed him further into the descent he was about to enter. But the nature of the lead up to his first killing was so strange, so hard to believe, that it too may have been the final catalyst that made the Columbian a killer.

When his wife walked out on him, Conde turned once more to prostitutes to satisfy his needs. It was after he had picked up one who went by the impressive name of Lazaro Comesana that, according to his lawyer, his life undertook another, unexpected and perturbing turn. It was while Conde was moving towards the sex that he thought he had paid for that he made a most unexpected discovery. He realised that Comesana was in fact not the attractive woman for whose services he thought he had paid, but a cross dressing male prostitute. At the time, Conde was working as a building supply salesman. While such a role is not perhaps as demanding as, say, being a doctor or lawyer, it does require more than a modicum of awareness.

Apparently, though. Conde was in such a pit of despair that he was able to mistake a male prostitute – even a cross dressing one – for a woman. One can only imagine the point at which his mistake became apparent, but Conde's response knocked any smutty sense of humour in the mistaken encounter firmly out of the ball park.

'His life fell apart when he went to a prostitute who turned out to be a man,' claimed Fink, not especially convincingly. A document filed at the trial explained in more detail Conde's hard to believe confusion.

'Rory explained that he killed Comesana out of his anger about Comesana's deception, and his believe that his wife and children had left him because of his use of prostitutes,' read the document. After his discovery about his victim's gender, Conde strangled Lazaro to death.

It is unclear whether the next statement issued at court referred to the time prior to or after the prostitute had been strangled. For Lazaro's sake, we must hope it was after he was already dead.

'He (Conde) described kneeling over Comesana's body for ten minutes while he blamed him for the loss of his wife and children. He then made the sign of the cross over Comesana's body.' Of course, whether these actions should be described as the momentary lapse of control from a man under severe emotional pressure, as the acts of one with mental illness or the work of a cold blooded and merciless killer is yet another of the questions in this case which remain impossible to answer with certainty.

However, what happened next is definitely unusual in crimes of this kind. Conde dressed his victim, loaded him into his car and drove him to an upmarket area off the Tamiami Trail. There, he threw the body out, leaving it to be found in the open close to the road. Something he would repeat five more times as his killing spree gathered pace. He made no attempt to hide the bodies, yet appeared to hold the sense of propriety to ensure his victims' decency.

His next victim followed very shortly after. On October 8th, 1994 he picked up prostitute Elisa Martinez. When her body was also found, dressed and strangled, once more just off the Tamiami Trail, police began to wonder whether they had a copycat killer on their hands, or a serial killer. Within another six weeks they were further perplexed when the strangled body of the next prostitute was found in a similar place. This time, however, the killer had gone further. A message had been left on the back and buttocks of the dead woman, Charity Nava. This message consisted of words written in flamboyant looped and flowing letters alongside almost childish symbols. The sort of writing which is popular with elementary school girls when writing messages to their best friends forever. However, the content of the missive engraved with black marker pen on Charity's back was anything but the normal kind of message sent by such children.

'Third,' it read. 'I will call Dwight Chan 10. See if you can catch me.'

The 'Third' appeared in bold capitals. Above the 'I' was an ungrammatical dot in the style of a smiley face. The reference to Dwight Chan refers to a WPLG TV anchor popular at the times, Dwight Lauderdale, who appeared on Channel Ten. The word 'See' was presented pictorially, using two circles to represent eyes. All this scrawled on the back of a murder victim. Clearly, the culprit was either somebody suffering from severe mental illness, who was completely unable to empathise with the women he was killing, or somebody filled with evil.

Conde remained in touch with Carla during this time in order to visit his children. However, she noted later how drawn and ill he looked, and how depressed he acted. He would often cry on his visits. He was invited to spend Thanksgiving with her family but left suddenly at 10.00pm without a thank you or goodbye. The following day, on November 25th, 1994, just five days after the murder of Charity, another body was discovered. Wanda Crawford had, it seemed, met the identical fate to her predecessors. Next on his list of victims was Necole Schneider, who died on December seventeenth. Then early in

1995, Conde demonstrated that he had not turned over a new leaf and adopted a New Year's resolution to end his murderous ways. Rhonda Dunn was his sixth and, as far as is known, final victim. She was killed on January 12th of that year. It should be noted that Conde's abuse of his victims frequently continued after their death. Some, at least, of his victims were raped anally after Conde had killed them. Necrophilia could be added to the list of charges against him.

The state of Conde's mental health is inevitably a big question when considering the extent of his moral guilt, even though his physical complicity cannot be questioned. A detective involved in the investigation and capture of Conde discovered that, after he had strangled his victims, Conde would engage in lengthy conversations with them. During these, he claimed, he would give them advice as to where they went wrong, and to explain that now they were 'his', they could get back on the straight and narrow.

Perhaps this strange approach explains to some extent why he redressed his victims before casting them aside.

There can be a tendency, and it was much stronger at the time of Conde's reign of terror, to somehow lessen the outrage one feels because his victims are prostitutes. Such a position is not admirable. Lazaro Comensana, Elisa Martinez, Charity Nava, Wanda Crawford, Necole Schneider and Rhonda Dunn were each a real, living person with their own hopes and dreams. Their own families, loves and stresses. That they had each found themselves on a path which included prostitution could have been for many reasons. Typically, we know less about these victims than so many others who died violently at the hands of different killers but were not prostitutes. Yet that does not mean that the occupation in which Conde's targets ended up is likely to have been the one they intended to choose.

Take Charity Nava as a sad example. Charity was just twenty-three years old when she died. There are no pages high up on internet search engines celebrating her life. Commiserating her death either. On one site sits a picture of a young, unhappy looking face, pain in her eyes beneath curly hair. More digits are given to her memorial ID – 133366686 for those who are interested – than her life. Her place of burial is listed as 'Unknown'. Her existence is summed up in under ten words. 'Charity fell prey to serial killer Rory Enrique Conde' states this minimal information. Who were her parents? What were her ambitions? Where would she be today had she not had the misfortune to be picked up by a slim man whose wife had recently left him?

We do not know. And that is as much a tragedy as the manner of her death. When Conde strangled her, he took away not only her life and her future, but her past as well.

However, whilst Conde did not kill any more prostitutes there was at least one more near fatality as he resumed his attacks. For some reason, there had been a brief lull in his activities. According to Conde, this was because he retained the hope that he could be reunited with his family. He did, however, claim to have committed two further rapes during this quieter period in his offending. Maybe an insight can be gained from other serial killer cases. Some killers are desperate to be caught, sensing this would be the only way they could bring to an end a spree which operated largely out of their control.

That was not the way Conde's mind worked. It is believed that he was actually paranoid about being caught, rather than not being found out. As local and national media became besotted by the killing rampage upon which some unknown felon was engaging, Conde may have decided the lie of the land was becoming too dangerous, too hot for further escapades.

That did not stop him, however, from engaging in other crimes. On June 19th, 1995 he was to be found in court facing a more minor charge of shoplifting. Meanwhile, back in his apartment, another victim lay bruised, assaulted, raped and battered. Gloria Maestra, though wrapped in duct tape, was determined to make herself heard, and managed to attract the attention of neighbors. The police were called, and Gloria was freed and shown the photographs in Conde's apartment. She immediately picked out her attacker. Police checked back on the limited evidence that they had regarding the crimes, and one small clue lay in the fact that the tyre marks found close to where a couple of the bodies had been discarded, alongside witness reports, suggested an old model Toyota Celica. Conde owned just such a vehicle. With two strong pieces of evidence now tying him to the crimes, the police swooped and the number one and only suspect was arrested.

Conde was tried first for the murder of Rhonda Dunn. He admitted the crime, but here made his claim that it was a combination of the childhood abuse he had suffered, the experience of having sex with a prostitute he thought was female but who was in fact a man and that his wife had left him that led to a breakdown in his mental state, causing him to kill Rhonda. While his attorney, and Conde, accepted that he had carried out both the murders of Rhonda and the other victims, the defense argued that he had neither premeditated nor planned his crimes.

The jury, though, did not buy his attorney's arguments, and on 20th October 1999 he was convicted of homicide and soon a recommendation of the death penalty was to follow. This was confirmed at a hearing which lasted just 45 minutes on March 17th, 2000. During that event, Conde appeared disinterested and sleepy, and said nothing in either mitigation or apology for what he had done.

Then, on April 5, 2001, he pleaded guilty to the murder of his remaining five victims. This was a part of a plea deal. Conde accepted the agreement which meant he would receive five consecutive life terms without the possibility of parole. Judge Jerald Bagley also required, as a part of the deal, that should Conde manage to get his single death penalty conviction overturned and converted to a lesser sentence, he could not use this as a springboard to change his position regarding the other convictions, and attempt to gain a release at any later stage in his life.

Katherine Fernandez Rundle was a Miami Dade State Attorney back then. 'This sentence will ensure that Rory Conde never again walks the streets of this community,' she said.

One puzzle of many that remain regarding Conde's actions relates to his motive for killing his victims. Although he was known to have been violent towards Clara, strangely he did not brutalise any of his victims with physical assaults. It is an often seen trait of serial killers that they do mutilate their targets, sometimes cutting them or dissecting their bodies, at other times savagely beating them. It is assumed that these killers gain some kind of satisfaction from their violence.

It seems likely that Conde gained satisfaction from the sex he had purchased, but felt he was doing society a service in removing prostitutes from the area around the Tamiami Trail on the outskirts of Miami where they proliferated. After all, he has always claimed that it was a prostitute who was responsible for destroying his marriage, and that was the trigger for his killing spree. It is a phenomenally self-serving standpoint for any person to adopt, especially one who has killed six and would no doubt have gone on to murder more had he not been caught. The major question such a position begs is an answer as to who was responsible for getting the prostitute in the first place? Clearly, in Conde's case, that was the man himself. However, rational thought is frequently not the strongest characteristic of either the mentally ill or serial killers. The fact is that if he genuinely held this view, then it could (in a highly circumspect way) be seen by Conde that he was, indeed, doing society some good. Nevertheless, the argument falls down to a large extent when it is considered that he still had the pleasure of the sex with his victims before killing them. Selfish altruism is an oxymoron of considerable contradiction, as is any concept of well intentioned homicide.

Deciding on a date to deliver a death sentence is a complex and long-lasting business. Nineteen years on, Conde awaits his fate. His crimes are undoubtedly vile, but there are surely enough doubts regarding his upbringing, and enough oddness in his behaviour, to suggest some kind of mitigating circumstances behind his obscene misdemeanours.

And so, Rory Conde sits in his cell on death row in the hot and humid State of Florida. He must be aware that a decision gets ever closer as each day passes. His is the strangest of cases; albeit one in which the evidence seems clear. He killed five women and a man he initially believed to be a woman. Of that there is no doubt. But so many questions remain regarding the killer. Was his childhood as damaging as is presented? Was he abused emotionally and sexually as a small boy? Does his self-serving way of rationalising his acts actually indicate a mental illness which should save him from the gurney, or just a selfishness with which he tries to justify the actions of an evil and merciless man?

In truth, we will never know for sure. There can be no doubt that Conde will never leave prison. Whether his death comes as a result of a lethal injection, or natural causes, is much more in the balance. Whatever the outcome, however, let us not lose sight of the suffering of his victims. Their stories are more important than his. It would be good if one day somebody is able to tell them.

RODNEY ALCALA

ZOE FOSTER

Rodney Alcala is a serial murderer that is most often referred to as the "Dating Game Killer" after he was a contestant on the popular game show "The Dating Game" in 1978

He was sentenced to death in California in 2010 for committing five murders in the state between 1977 and 1979. It is believed, however, that he may have over 130 victims.

Alcala's charisma and murderous output have a striking similarity to that of Ted Bundy. More than one police detective has referred to him as a "killing machine." He was a sexual sadist and specialized in strangling as a form of torture. He would choke his victims into unconsciousness then revive them only to repeat the torture again.

He specialized in creating false photo auditions in which he would book prospective models for a photo shoot then rape and kill them. A traveling serial killer, Alcala would operate out of the Los Angeles area but would journey as far as the Pacific Northwest in search of victims. He would have a locker in Seattle where he would keep a stash of mementos and photographs of his victims.

In September of 2016, authorities released a series of photographs that they believe could be additional victims of Alcala. They are now asking for the public's help in identifying who the subjects in the photos are.

A KILLER IS BORN

Alcala was born in San Antonio, Texas to Raul Buquor and Anna Gutierrez in August of 1943. Rodney would live with his two sisters, one brother, mother, father and maternal grandmother in the middle-class San Antonio neighborhood. He had one older brother, Roy, who was born in 1941. Paqui, his older sister would be born in 1942. Then came Rodney, in 1943 and his younger sister Krissy in 1947.The family would enjoy cookouts, picnics, and the zoo. There were no indications of abuse or abnormal behavior of anyone.

Alcala would be sent to a Catholic school where he was reported to have been an excellent student. His polite and respectful manner would put him into good grace with his teachers who gave him top marks.

The family was a happy one until around 1951. This would be the year that Alcala's grandmother would fall ill. She wanted to live out her final years in her native Mexico. Seeking to grant her mother's dying wish, Alcala's mother would convince her husband to move the family to Mexico.

The family enjoyed the rural surroundings and the company from a loving extended family. Alcala would continue to excel in school, getting good grades at the American school in Mexico. But his grandmother would eventually die and his parents would split up. His father would abandon the family and move to California.

In 1954, Alcala's mother decided to move the family back to the United States. They would settle in Los Angeles but once again, Alcala and his siblings adjusted well.

At the age of thirteen, Alcala would attend St. Alphonsus in East Los Angeles where he would remain for two years. Now entering high school, he would enroll at the private Cantwell-Sacred Heart of Mary.

A CHANGE OF HEART

In an odd move, Alcala felt he had enough of Catholic teachings and wanted to attend public school for his final semester. He begged his mother to let him switch and after much cajoling, she granted him permission to change schools.

An excited Alcala would then attend Montebello High School for the last half of his senior year.

"Alcala gave no indication of a future serial killer," forensic psychologist Paula Orange said. "He was popular, well-liked and had gone out with a lot of girls. He looked completely well-adjusted."

Alcala enjoyed his senior year to the hilt. He played piano, lettered in cross country and was on the yearbook planning committee. He graduated near the head of his class in 1960.

Upon graduating Alcala decided to follow in the footsteps of his brother Roy who was at West Point. Alcala joined the army on June 19th, 1961 completing his family legacy of military service.

Alcala would be transferred to Ft. Bragg in North Carolina with the intention of becoming a paratrooper. In the interim, he would serve as a clerk and receive good marks from his military superiors. Alcala would keep his family abreast with letters of his adventures in the military but would rarely call home.

In 1962, Rodney's father would die in Tulare County, in California. He was 55 years old and was working as a Spanish language instructor. The death was described as "unexpected". Both he and his brother would be excused from their military duties in order to attend his funeral.

A CHANGE IN PERSONALITY

Alcala would serve without incident in the Army for four years without incident. But when he turned twenty-one, something inside his head snapped. He would suffer a "nervous breakdown" in 1964 and escape from the Army base.

Alcala ended up hitch-hiking all the way from Ft. Bragg, North Carolina to his mother's home in Monterey Park, California.

His mother expressed shock when Rodney ended up at her doorstep. He was anxious and disheveled.

Alcala then told his mother what he had done and that he had gone AWOL. She warned him of the consequences of his actions and insisted that he turn himself in. He then went to the local recruiting station and informed them of his AWOL status.

His mother worried. She had never seen her son in such a bizarre mental state. The military psychiatrist would diagnose him with an antisocial personality disorder. The U.S. Army would then discharge him from the service.

"Whether Alcala really suffered from a 'nervous breakdown' is open to conjecture," Orange said. "When he wanted to get out of something, he would find a way. Something happened at the Catholic school he attended where he wanted out. So he manipulated his mother into sending him to a public school. In the Army, he clearly wanted out so he figured out a way to cut loose. Acting crazy was one way of achieving his goal."

A NEW IDENTITY

On the surface, Alcala would seemingly find himself during his time as a student at UCLA. He took photography classes and ended up getting a Bachelor's degree in Fine Arts. His IQ was reported as genius level, around 135-140, and he graduated with honors. Everyone who met Alcala during his tenure at UCLA was impressed with his intelligence and determination to pursue his "art."

Alcala's first reported attack would occur in 1968 when he was twenty-five years old. He lured an eight-year-old girl walking to school in Hollywood into his car and brought her back to his apartment on De Longpre Avenue. An alert passerby would spot him entice the girl into his car and called the police.

LAPD would arrive at his home and demand that he open up. Alcala opened the door, shirtless and calm, informing police that he would "be right with them."

The officers waited a few minutes before realizing that had been duped. They entered the residence and inside they would find an unconscious little girl on the floor. She had been raped and had her head smashed in with a pipe.

Alcala had escaped through a back door, a fugitive on the run for the next three years.

Retired detective Steve Hodel had caught the case. He remembered how Alcala would be described as a smooth-talking, polite man by those around him.

"You have the wrong guy," one of Alcala's UCLA art professors insisted to Hodel as he investigated the killer's background. "He wouldn't hurt a fly."

Hodel's investigation would go nowhere for three years. But then he would get a break from the FBI in that they would put Alcala on the Ten Most Wanted List. The posters were spread nationwide and two teenage girls in New Hampshire would recognize the man in the "Wanted" sign.

They knew him as John or "Burger", their counselor at an acting camp called New Beginnings, located in Georges Mills, New Hampshire.

Panicked, the girls would notify the dean who contacted the authorities.

ART SCHOOL POSEUR

Alcala had spent the last three years reinventing himself as "John Berger" or "John Burger" on the East Coast art scene. He changed his name, got a new ID and attended NYU film classes like he did at UCLA.

Alcala knew how to play the artsy-fartsy game, with his educational background in arts and film. After his release from prison, he would reenter that world as he targeted young and attractive women.

His first reported murder victim would be Cornelia 'Michael' Crilley in 1971. Crilley was the middle child of an Irish family with five children. She had a middle name of Michelle which morphed into "Michael" as she grew up in the boroughs of Queens in New York City.

Unfortunately, the police would suspect Crilley's boyfriend, Leon Borstein, of her murder. Borstein had been an assistant district attorney in Brooklyn at the time. Her murder would remain unsolved for decades.

"I am now almost seventy-one," Borstein said. "And this occurred forty years ago, and I am still affected by it. I was crazy about her at the time. ... I was devastated by her death. She was beautiful, charming, with a great sense of humor. She had the Irish eyes and the Irish hair."

Borstein believed that somehow Crilley met Alcala while she was moving furniture into her new apartment.

"He just repeated out there," Hodel said. "He was a class-A con man and I recognized how dangerous he was. He was able to con people as an intelligent, refined person — and that is a dangerous combination."

Alcala would be arrested on August 12th, 1971 and transported back to Los Angeles to face rape charges of the eight-year-old "Tali", a pseudonym giving to his eight-year-old victim.

"I have been trying to forget what happened," Alcala said under the interrogation of Hodel. "I have forgotten all about Rod Alcala and what he did."

Unfortunately, Alcala was captured during a time period in which brutally raping a child in the state of California would not be assured of a long jail term. The California state government still believed that rapists could be rehabilitated through therapy and education.

"My impression was that it was his first sex crime, and we got him early — and society is relatively safe now," Retired LAPD Detective Steve Hodel said. "I had no idea in two years (Alcala would be free) and continue his reign of terror and horror. I expected he was put away and society was safe. ... It is such a tragedy that so much more came after that."

Because of the lenient court system, Alcala would serve only thirty-four months for the rape of the eight-year-old "Tali".

BI-COASTAL KILLER

Alcala found himself a free man in 1974 and now began touring the communities of Southern California looking for victims. He would be arrested for giving pot to a minor (a thirteen-year-old known in the court records as 'Julie J') who later stated that he had kidnapped her.

She told police that Alcala had forced her to smoke marijuana and tried to kiss her. Alcala would be arrested but once again the liberal laws of California went easy on him. He would go back to jail and serve less than two years. Convinced of his "rehabilitation," his parole officer would then okay a visit for Alcala to go to New York to "visit relatives."

Upon arrival, Alcala would stalk and kill Ellen Hover.

Ellen was a socialite and a piano virtuoso, daughter of Herman Hover who owned the famed nightclub Ciro's. Friends would describe her as "naive, sheltered and trusting." Pictures reveal Ellen as model beautiful, with long brown hair and a shy smile.

Her disappearance went send shockwaves throughout the tight-knit New York social elite. Police would search her apartment and find a name she scrawled on her calendar the day she vanished.

The name was "John Berger", Alcala's alias.

Her disappearance coincided with the Son of Sam serial killings in New York and it drew the attention of the FBI. Ellen's father Herman was a man of means and influence (he counted Sammy Davis Jr and Dean Martin as friends) who immediately hired the best private investigator available.

The private detective would discover that Ellen was last seen with a "pony-tailed photographer" who people referred to as "John Burger". They connected the dots but could not find Alcala.

Ellen's skeletal remains would later be found buried in the wooded area of the Rockefeller Estate.

"Ellen was [found] wearing my T-shirt," Ellen's sister Victoria said. "My parents had a weekend house 10 minutes away. ... She was my role model. I wanted to be just like her. ... I am devastated, and to this day it is very hard. It ripped our family apart."

NYPD continued to look for "John Burger", but Alcala returned to Los Angeles in 1977. He used his own name while getting a job at the Los Angeles Times as a typesetter. There he would be the man who set up the articles describing his own killings for print.

ROAD TRIP TO SEATTLE?

Alcala seemingly picked places at random for his killings. For whatever reason, he would pick Seattle as one of his killing fields. He set up a locker there where he would keep mementos of his crime, a storage unit where he his darkest secrets could be kept under lock and key.

His first known victim in Seattle would be Antoinette Witaker.

Antoinette was known by her family and friends as "Tony" . She was a tough girl that would fight with her mom and run away from home. But she also wrote poetry and had a romantic streak. She was thirteen years old when she walked out the door of a foster home with "an unknown man with long-reddish colored hair" on the night of July 9th, 1977.

Her dead body would be found a week later She would be fully clothed, propped up on her hands and knees in a vacant lot in Lake City, Washington. She had been dead for over a week.

Antoinette had been stabbed to death but there was no evidence that she had been sexually assaulted. Her mother, Barbara Oliver, would argue vociferously that her daughter's murder wasn't a priority because she was black.

A SEASON OF SERIAL KILLERS

Alcala operated at the same time Southern Californians were being terrorized by the Hillside Strangler murders. Bodies of young women were being left in ravines and woodsy areas. Alcala operated under a similar modus operandi.

Alcala would return to Los Angeles and kill Jill Barcomb. Her murder would later be falsely attributed to the Hillside Stranglers because her body was found on an abandoned road near Marlon Brando's home (which was near other killings of the Hillside Stranglers.)

Alcala had posed Barcomb's dead body in a fetal position, like a photographer directing a model.

Jill Barcomb was described as a "runaway" by her brother, Bruce Barcomb. She had grown up in a Catholic family and was the fifth child of eleven kids.

"Her death put a tremendous hole in my life," Bruce said. "My life changed dramatically. She took me to my first freshman dance. She played trumpet in the high school band. She was a candy striper. She was not a throwaway kid."

Jill Barcomb had attended Oneida High School and was slated to graduate in 1977. Family members remember as having had a bit of a wild side but she was "a bubbly little girl" according to her aunt Arlene.

"She was just a tiny little thing that couldn't have weighed more than 90 pounds," Jill's aunt, Arlene Barcomb said.

It is unknown how she got into the cross hairs of Alcala.

After her body was found, police began scouring the Los Angeles neighborhood. They interviewed everyone, including Marlon Brando, but no one had seen anything.

Two months later, in December of 1977, Alcala would be brought into LAPD's Parker Center to be interviewed by the FBI. They didn't connect him to Barcomb's killing, however, but they connected the dots to another angle.

He was identified as the "John Burger" who had been at the New Directions acting camp that had been arrested for the Tali rape case. He could also be the same "John Burger" who Ellen Hover had written on her calendar.

Alcala was interrogated and he admitted that he had become acquainted with Ellen Hover. They could not get him to confess, however. Ellen's body still had not been found so they had to release him.

Two days later, Alcala would kill again.

This time, it would be 27-year-old Georgia Wixted, a blonde cardiac care nurse with model good looks.

Georgia was the middle child raised by a widowed mother. Her mother worked to provide for the family while Georgia and her brother Michael would care for their younger sister, Anne. Georgia had been a sickly teenager, hospitalized twice for surgery to remove tumors. It was her experience during her hospital stay that made her want to become a nurse.

STALKING

The night before her murder, Georgia attended a birthday party at the Brennan's Pub in Santa Monica.

On December 16th, 1977, her naked body would be found inside her Malibu apartment. She had been raped, strangled and beaten with a hammer.

"No one should have to die the way my sister did," her sister Anne said. "No one should have to suffer that way."

"Alcala thought he could get away with anything," forensic psychologist Paula Orange said. "It was his way of showing he was the boss. But he left some evidence behind. A clear half-print of his palm and his DNA on Georgia's window."

Georgia's sister Anne would later reveal that she has had a lifetime of nightmares over her sister's death. She learned of the murder with a phone call and gets anxious every time the phone rings. She never feels safe and always looks over her shoulder.

"And then there is the emptiness," Anne said. "The empty chair at the dinner table; the empty bed in my room. The holidays that would come and go and feel empty."

Her mother could not cope with the loss of Georgia. She would be hospitalized for psychiatric care after the murder and would suffer from depression for the rest of her life.

A KILLER ON THE MOVE

Alcala would take special care to not strike in the same vicinity twice. His murders would seemingly be random, he would select a woman that caught his eye then stalk them out. He would change his location, however, and because of the lack of technology in the 1970s, the authorities would have trouble connecting the dots.

With that thought process in mind, Alcala would then travel to the Bay Area.

Pamela Lambson would capture his eye, another young and well-proportioned young woman. Lambson was a computer assistant, singer and aspiring actress.

Lambson would disappear from Fisherman's Wharf in San Francisco on October 8, 1977, after she would go to meet a "freelance photographer."

"This may be my big chance," Pamela would tell her friend after she met a pony-tailed stranger at Fisherman's Wharf for a photo shoot." He had promised the blonde and bubbly actress a series of glamour pictures but instead raped and murdered her.

Lambson's body would be found the next day on a trail on Mount Tamalpais in Marin County.

"He took my precious daughter's life," Pamela's mother, Jean Lambson said. "And we were all crippled by it. I felt so devastated that I wanted to die. If I could just die, I wouldn't have to feel this pain. It was so intense, I could hardly bear it. But I had to get out of that depression because I had four beautiful sons and a husband to take care of. My daughter is gone for now, but we will see her again, we will be able to be together again."

After murdering Lambson, Alcala would take a road trip to Wyoming. There he would meet Christine Thornton, a 28-year old woman who was six months pregnant.

Alcala would bury her in a ranch in Granger, Wyoming. Thornton would be a missing person for five years until her body was uncovered by a rancher in 1982. Her link to Alcala would not be known for decades. It wasn't until police revealed photos years later that they realized that Thornton was one of the models in his portfolio.

Thornton's sister, Kathy, would discover her in an on-line set of photos wherein the authorities wanted the public's help in identifying the women. Alcala had photographed Thornton sitting atop a Kawasaki 500 motorcycle. She wore a yellow top, flip-flops and looked to be six months pregnant.

Pretty and smiling, she had no idea who that the man taking the picture was the epitome of evil.

A RETURN TO THE KILL SITE

Alcala would take another road trip to Seattle, perhaps to both relive his killing of Antoinette Walker and to seek fresh victims.

This time, he would meet the developmentally disabled Joyce Gaunt.

Gaunt's body would be found on February 17th, 1978 at a picnic area at Seward Park. She had been beaten, strangled and raped.

Gaunt had been living in a group home on Capitol Hill in Seattle. Local media had little to say about Gaunt' murder and Seattle true-crime writer Ann Rule described Gaunt as "trusting as a child of 8 or 10."

It was the night of February 16th, 1978 that Gaunt had called her group home around midnight. She was told to come home but she didn't want to and hung up the phone.

No one knows why she was in the park.

The next morning, her nude body had been found lying face first in the dirt, her skull crushed.

BACK IN LOS ANGELES

Upon his return to Los Angeles, Alcala would be detailed as part of an LAPD round-up of all sex offenders. They wanted desperately to find the Hillside Strangler and Alcala came up as a possible suspect. They would find him at his mother's home in March of 1978.

After questioning, however, Alcala would be ruled out as the Strangler. But officers would frisk him and find marijuana in his pants. He would be jailed for a brief period.

THE DATING GAME

Now with numerous cross-country murders on his resume, Alcala inexplicably became a contestant on The Dating Game. He was a registered sex offender so once again it is a head-scratcher as to how he got past the screening process.

Host Jim Lange would introduce Alcala as "Bachelor Number One" and describe him as "a successful photographer who got his start when his father found him in the darkroom at the age of 13, fully developed. Between takes, you might find him skydiving or motorcycling."

Alcala would be one of three bachelors vying for a date with Cheryl Bradshaw. Bradshaw would ask Alcala to give his best impression of a "dirty old man".

Alcala would then grunt and groan, saying "come on over here."

The audience would laugh.

"I am serving you for dinner," Bradshaw said. "What would you like?"

"I am called the Banana," Alcala responded. "And I look pretty good."

"Be more descriptive."

"Peel me," Alcala said.

Alcala would win the contest but ultimately Cheryl Bradshaw would not go out with him. She thought he was "creepy" upon meeting him.

One of his fellow contestants, Jed Mills, would later describe him as a "very strange guy" with "bizarre opinions."

REJECTION AND ITS AFTERMATH

Alcala's rampage would continue as he would seemingly need to find a woman who resembled Cheryl Bradshaw. He would find that woman in Santa Monica legal secretary Charlotte Lamb.

Lamb's body would be found posed nude, laying face up with her arms behind her back. Detective Cliff Shepard believes that Alcala did things like this "to defile the victims as best as he can in death."

She had been strangled with a shoelace.

Charlotte Lamb was the fourth in a family of eight children born to tenant farmers in Ohio. She had long blonde hair and everyone called her "Shug". She painted, sang, made skirts and dresses.

After high school, she would leave Ohio and head to Los Angeles with a boyfriend. On Charlotte's 32nd birthday, her sister Celia Adkins, would call her again and again throughout the day and get no answer. She didn't know that days earlier, on June 24, 1978, Charlotte's naked body had been found in the laundry room of her apartment complex in El Segundo.

Her family did not learn of her death until weeks later.

TAKING SOUVENIRS

Alcala would take Lamb's earrings as a trophy in the murder. Her mother had to be hospitalized after she learned that her daughter had been beaten, bitten, raped and strangled.

"He wanted it as a memento," Orange said. "He could look at the earring and relive the moments of his attack, getting a thrill. Taking 'trophies' is a way a serial killer can relive his thrills."

"The ripple effect of her loss has taken a toll on each family member," Charlotte's sister Carolyn said. "We've been robbed of hearing her cute laugh when she'd call every month and chat many times for over an hour. The giant hole created when she was taken from us will never be filled."

MOMMA'S BOY

In 1979, a fifteen-year-old hitch-hiker would call police from a motel in Riverside County to report that she had just escaped from a kidnapper and rapist. Police would arrive on scene and arrest Alcala, the judge would set his bail at just $10,000.

But Alcala's mother would race to the rescue, paying the bail and setting her son free.

Later, Huntington Beach detectives also suspected another of Alcala's female family members of trying to hide a receipt to his locker in Seattle.

Now out on bail, Alcala would then kill twenty-one-year-old computer keypunch operator Jill Parenteau.

It was the summer of 1979, and Jill Parenteau had turned twenty-one . She was excited about moving out on her own. She had long brown hair and a big smile, was smart and funny but was shy around those she didn't know well.

Her childhood friend Katherine Franco remembered her as a friend where they did "classic girlfriend things." They would cook, shop and talk about where life would take them. They then visit the Handlebar Saloon, a Pasadena bar that Alcala would visit a lot. They only talked with him briefly and he made little impression on them.

But Alcala would follow Parenteau home and sneak into her apartment as she slept on June 14th, 1979. Alcala would climb through her window but cut himself. He had a rare blood type which police would later match to the blood remains on the broken glass.

"I think how Jill must have felt safe in her apartment, in her own bed," Jill's sister, Dedee Parenteau said. "Then this evil monster appeared. She fought for her life. The terror she must have felt. It sickens me, it breaks my heart, knowing the last face she saw in her life was that of this monster."

"There is no closure. I can't have her back, can't erase what she had to endure in her final moments. Nothing will end this nightmare."

A KILLING MACHINE

Six days after Parenteau was murdered, Robin Samsoe would disappear.

It was a kidnapping that shocked the safe, quiet Southern California community where she lived. Samsoe's friend, Bridget, would tell police that the two bikini-clad girls were asked by a man with a camera if he could take their picture. A suspicious neighbor came to the rescue, scaring off Alcala.

Bridget then lent Robin her yellow bike so that she could make it on time to her ballet class. It would be the last time anyone would ever see Robin Samsoe alive again.

Twelve days after she disappeared, Samsoe's body would be found by forest rangers. Bridget would describe the photographer to authorities, however, and a sketch would be shown everywhere in the media. A parole officer would recognize Alcala from the sketches and notify the police. Three weeks after Samsoe's body was found, Alcala would be arrested at his mother's home in Monterey Park.

Police had finally tripped up Alcala. The killer would state that he had been applying at Knott's Berry Farm applying for a job as a photographer for a disco contest. Police had already searched his home, however, and they found a receipt for a locker in Seattle.

Authorities immediately flew to Seattle and opened his locker. Inside, they found photos of numerous young girls. He had been stalking some of them, taking their pictures. The also found a photo of Lorraine Werts, a girl who posed for him in the same neighborhood where he had approached Bridget and Robin. They also found Robin's gold ball earrings inside as well as rose earrings with DNA that they would later match to Charlotte Lamb.

A BITTER ENDING

Alcala would finally be arrested, tried and convicted only to have the verdict overturned several times. Finally, in 2013, he would be convicted of 25 years to life for the third time.

"I don't have any faith in the system," Robert Samsoe said (he was thirteen when his baby sister was Robin killed.) "Some people, they are just afforded all the chances in the world. Alcala has cost the state of California more than any other person because of his lawsuits. And they treat him like a king. Everybody is walking on pins and needles around him. He has had 30 years to study the law on death row. He is afforded that right."

The murder of Robert's younger sister would emotionally cripple the Samsoe family. Robert would himself become a "deeply troubled young man" according to an article in LA Weekly.

"It takes me everything I have to not jump over the chairs and grab him by the head and smash his head into the table," Samsoe said when asked about Alcala's new trial. "That is what I think about. The worst part of it is that you have to tell your kids, 'I can protect you,' but in your heart, you know that there are monsters out there — and you really can't."

PICTURES OF UNKNOWN WOMEN

In March of 2010, both the Huntington Beach and New York City police department released 120 of Alcala's photographs on-line. They wanted the public's help in identifying some of the women and children in the photographs. In the first month, over twenty-one women came forward and identified themselves in the pictures. Six families came forward and recognized loved ones who had disappeared during the 1970s. With the exception of Christine Thornton, however, the rest of the identifications remain unsolved.

In September of 2016, police would release another 110 photos and would ask again for the public's help in identifying them.

More than 800 photographs of Alcala's photographs would remain classified as the police have deemed them as too "sexually explicit."

KILLER HANDYMAN

JOLENE DEAN

It was February of 1955 in Toronto, Canada. The temperatures averaged sixteen degrees Fahrenheit and citizens were cozied up in their homes for the time being. At the time, immigrants were moving into the neighborhoods and what was once a quiet, peaceful city was beginning to turn into a bonafide metropolis. On the twenty-seventh of that month, a little boy was born to two parents. However, his biological father disappeared not long after his birth and was never to be heard from again. His mother struggled for three years to keep food on the table for her and her son, and then his aunt finally intervened. She being a recluse, there isn't much known about the boy's time with his aunt.

There are stories about him as a child that painted him as a quiet boy who often made other children feel uneasy, but they didn't have a specific reason as to why. When he became of age and was able to trek out on his own, he took odd jobs here and there as a traveling handyman. Unfortunately, young William was not able to stay away from a life of petty crime that quickly grew into a life of savagery.

He reconnected with his mother in his early thirties, but did not have contact with her before that point as far as the police and investigators know. Many suspect something terrible happened during William's childhood to make him who he is today, but there are no records of abuse or neglect while he was under the care of his aunt. In fact, many believe she instilled some very good qualities in him as a boy. William would not have been able to become the independent handyman he'd been in his twenties if she had not.

Despite his life of small, petty crimes, William was a successful handyman.

It was at the age of twenty-two when his life took a notable turn. According to court records and newspapers, William was convicted for several different charges. He was convicted of abduction, breaking and entering, theft, and pretending to solemnize a marriage. In addition, he was convicted of libel, or a written defamation.

The cause of this change in his behavior? William Fyfe had begun to experiment with drugs. He would later seek counseling for this addiction, but it was never clear if he actually was able to become clean or if he was just able to control his actions while he was under the influence. William would find odd jobs here and there to fuel his drug habit, and if those jobs dried up, he resorted to robbery.

After Fyfe was released for the aforementioned crimes, he began a wanderer. He lived in several different cities across Canada until he finally settled in with his biological mother.

He appeared to be a normal individual who didn't harbor any murderous tendencies, but the mother of one of his hockey buddies soon learned this was untrue. William's murderous ways began in 1979 with Hazel Scattolon, but it wouldn't be until the late nineties that he was finally arrested and charged with her death, as well as four more deaths. If these were the only crimes he'd committed, he wouldn't be considered the deadliest serial killer Canada has ever seen, but there is evidence to suggest William has been a part of numerous other crimes over the twenty years between Hazel's murder and the murders of Anna Yarnold, Monique Gaudreau, Teresa Shanahan, and Mary Glen.

If this is the case, then he would be classified as the deadliest serial killer of Canada, but unfortunately, William Fyfe is rather tight-lipped about his involvement in the open cases.

Let's explore the life of William Fyfe and what it is that made him one of Canada's most frightening criminals.

Chapter One – The Beginning of the End

William Fyfe was not pegged as a suspect for the first few murders he committed, nor was he a suspect in the serial rapes that took place in the 1980's that he later claimed he committed. What was his ultimate downfall were the murders that took place in the 1990's, beginning with a woman named Anna Yarnold.

Anna Yarnold

It was an average winter in October of 1999 for Senneville, Quebec. The neighborhood was peaceful and the police were not accustomed to handling violent crime. With around 1,500 residents, it was quite clear the occupants of this peaceful town knew one another well.

Her neighbors and living relatives described Anna Yarnold as an artistic woman who enjoyed painting and making flower arrangements. Her daughter describes her as being a spontaneous woman who was very much into life. Unfortunately, it was cut short.

In October of 1999, Anna lived in Senneville, Quebec, a quiet, peaceful area the police considered an easygoing place to work due to the little amount of violent crime they witnessed. The population was around fifteen hundred people, with the area being secluded and wooded. Mrs. Yarnold's home was located off the beaten path where the only thing to be seen from the windows were trees. Her home was private and secluded, making her an easy target, unfortunately.

The day Mrs. Yarnold was murdered was like any other day in Senneville, Quebec. Anna was worried about the health of her dog, Trooper, and took him to the local veterinarian at three in the afternoon. She'd noticed a lump on his side and was very worried about him. Her veterinarian informed her Trooper's lump could be cancerous and they had to remove it. After the appointment, Anna took Trooper home to her secluded, waterfront home.

Worried about his wife, Robert Yarnold called her from work to check in on her and Trooper shortly after they arrived home. Her daughter called her around five thirty in the afternoon and noticed her mother sounded as if she'd been crying. They talked for quite some time about Trooper, and Sarah Yarnold tried to calm her mother. Both her husband and her daughter assured her everything would be okay with Trooper, and that was the last either one of them spoke with her.

As darkness fell over the providence of Montreal, West Island, an unexpected visitor approached Anna Yarnold's home in a pickup truck. On October 15, 1999, the following morning, her daughter and husband both tried calling her multiple times because they were worried about her emotional well-being concerning Trooper. By that time, it was too late.

Both repeatedly attempted to reach the fifty-nine-year-old woman. As the evening set in on October 15, Robert Yarnold drove up this wife's home. The first thing he noticed about her home was the lights were on and her vehicle was in the driveway. Worried and curious, Robert went inside her home to look for his wife and her dog. He first searched the downstairs rooms but quickly made his way up to the upstairs bedrooms. In a guest bedroom, he found Trooper alive and well. On the bed, he found signs of possible foul play.

His wife's purse was on the spare bedroom's bed and her wallet was open. Her cards were strewn about and her change was emptied out across the bed. Worried, Robert decided to search for his wife. Finally, he made his way downstairs and out into the yard. Just outside a screened in porch near a triangular flower bed, he found his wife's body. She was lying face down, and when he turned her, it was obvious she had been murdered.

Robert Yarnold called the police, who arrived at the scene within an hour, and amongst them was a forensic photographer who took pictures of the scene. In the case file, it was noted she had bruises on her neck and around her face and severe head wounds. An officer found the flowerpot with blood caked on it and they labeled this as the murder weapon, but they were unable to get fingerprints due to the flowerpot's rough texture.

As police walked through the scene, they pieced together a possible chain of events.

Anna was attacked in her bathroom, where they found her glasses in the sink. It was clear she put up a fight, but he soon caught up with her outside and choked her before he beat her with the flowerpot. Once he was sure she was dead, he went back inside and stole what he was able to from her purse. While it appeared to be a robbery at first, police were suspicious of the obvious overkill.

When it comes to persons of interest in a case such as this, police often look at the victim's family members first. The closest family member is always the one who is scrutinized before anyone else, and in this case, it was Robert Yarnold. Robert was taken to the police station for questioning before his daughter, Sarah, was notified. She didn't know of the news yet and was called by her father around midnight.

Sarah was already worried about her mother and wanted to know what was happening, but her father wouldn't tell her over the phone. He told her was at the police station in St. Charles, and she immediately went there. She could see her father through the glass door of a conference room, but she was not able to go inside and speak with him. The police took Sarah to another room and began to ask her questions about the relationship her parents had together. Eventually, one of the officers blurted out to Sarah that her mother was dead. She describes the incident as shocking, but she didn't really believe what they were saying and couldn't believe her mother was dead. From the first moment she knew, she believed her father had not committed the crime.

Still, Robert was questioned late into the night but was only considered a person of interest at the time and not a suspect. Sarah and her father assumed it was a robbery, but the police began to say something completely different. The forensic scientist came up with absolutely nothing as they continued to search for clues. They searched her purse for fingerprints and the murder weapon. They searched the halls and the bathroom where they knew the suspect had been.

Nothing they were able to find helped them in the case of Anna Yarnold. Forensics had a difficult time finding anything that was of use because it was a murder committed by an outsider, making it difficult to look for anything that might be out of the ordinary.

Needless to say, the community was disturbed and frightened when the news was released about Anna Yarnold's death. There wasn't a clear motive as to why it happened, frightening her neighbors and those who knew her even more. She was a woman who was dearly loved in her community, and while some suspected her husband, others feared something much worse. If it was a stranger who committed this crime, then they could be next.

The police feared it was part of a much larger problem. Just three months prior, another violent incident had taken place.

Janet Kuchinsky

Somewhere in the files of the Montreal Police Station's Major Crimes Division rests a folder with the name Janet Kuchinsky. Unfortunately, her file rests in the cold case section. Janet was a forty-two-year-old mother of three who was bludgeoned to death off a bicycle path at the north end of Sources Boulevard in Pierrefonds on July 10, 1999. No one has been charged with her murder.

After six in the evening on July 10th, Janet left her home to go out on one of her frequent walks. According to the reports, police suspect she was killed shortly after she left. Her body was found the following day. No sexual assault had taken place and theft was ruled out because there was nothing missing. During the course of the investigation, numerous tips were followed but they all led to nothing.

A twenty-thousand dollar reward was posted for information leading to the arrest of a suspect, but it went unclaimed. If the murder of Janet and Anna were connected, it would have tipped the police off to a serial killer. The police advised everyone in the area not to answer the door to people they didn't know.

In the meantime, Robert Yarnold fully cooperated with the police, but it still wasn't good enough at the time. In the weeks that followed, there were no new attacks, but two new crimes in different areas caught the police's attention.

Chapter Two – The Murder of Monique Gaudreau and Teresa Shanahan

Fyfe was just getting started when he killed Anna Yarnold. The violence of her death pales in comparison to the violence Monique Gaudreau and Teresa Shanahan experienced.

Monique Gaudreau

Monique was a forty-five-year-old nurse who worked in Sainte-Agathe-des-Monts, Quebec and was described as being kind and caring to her patients. She wasn't one to be late for work or to miss her shift. On October 29, 1999, two weeks after Anna Yarnold was murdered, Monique failed to show up for her shift. Her coworkers and employer were concerned about her whereabouts and called her home multiple times. When they were unable to reach her, they contacted her sister who decided to drive to her home that evening.

Inside, Monique's sister found a gruesome discovery. The amount of violence at the scene shocked even the most seasoned veterans. Monique had been badly beaten across the head and face, and she had been stabbed multiple times. At one point during the struggle, she had been sexually assaulted. The police were unable to determine how many stab wound had been inflicted, but they estimated over fifty. It was evident to them the killer was a very sick-minded individual.

At this murder, a biologist was called to the scene to search for clues. The forensic photographer took photographs of the excessive amount of blood scattered across the walls in order to preserve the scene before the biologist was able to begin working. The police discovered few clues inside the home despite the attack being so brutal.

They were unable to find signs of forced entry, meaning Monique had opened her door to the intruder. They did not find a murder weapon, so the murderer must have taken it with him. There were not any fingerprints, and there was nothing missing from the scene. Only when they moved to the outside landing near the front porch did their search finally pay off.

A footprint was able to be pulled from the scene. They knew it was the killer's because it was in Monique's blood. What they also discovered was droplets of blood that led away from the scene, meaning the killer had hurt himself during the altercation. Usually, when an attacker goes after a victim with that much violence, they end up slipping and cutting themselves or hurting themselves with the weapon they're using.

The biologist determined the blood belonged to a male suspect, but nothing else was able to be gleaned from the scene. Because there was not a similar cause of death, the connection between Anna and Monique were not made until William Fyfe was caught.

The police knew they were getting closer to a suspect, but they weren't close enough. The blood came up with nothing in their database.

Teresa Shanahan

On November 19, 1999, three weeks after Monique as discovered murdered, employees at a local firm in Laval, Quebec were concerned about the absence of their accountant. Teresa Shanahan was a fifty-five-year-old woman who lived alone in an apartment complex. When her coworkers and the police finally arrived at her apartment, the first thing they saw was three or four newspapers stacked in front of her door.

Suspicious, the police had the concierge open the door. What they found was as gruesome as the murder of Monique. Teresa was found dead in her apartment. Evidence suggested she had been sexually assaulted and beaten before she was stabbed thirty-two times. The murder had a striking resemblance to Monique Gaudreau's. However, there was something different about this one.

There were items missing from her apartment. Bank cards and jewelry were missing. One of her bank cards were used at an ATM shortly after her estimated time of death. The perpetrator had emptied out her savings account, making one five hundred dollar withdrawal before midnight and one after. The police immediately had the security footage from the bank confiscated to review it for a suspect.

The person they saw in the video was definitely not Teresa. It was a man, but they were only able to see him from above and behind, so identification was impossible. However, it was clear the man knew her PIN number for the bank card.

Across the providence, Sarah Yarnold was making a discovery of her own. She was skimming through her mother's financial records when she noticed something untoward. Someone had withdrawn money on the day of her mother's death. Police immediately secured a security tape from the ATM on the day of Anna Yarnold's death. The man in the video was facing the camera, but he was wearing a hood that made it difficult to determine who he was. However, the police were able to determine the man in the video was around five foot ten and Caucasian with a beard.

There was one thing that was certain. The man in the video was not Robert Yarnold, and this cleared his name from the investigation. While there was relief on Sarah and Robert's side, there was dread on the police's. They knew at this point they might be dealing with a serial killer.

It was clear to them, after discovering Teresa, that the man had used torture in order to get the women to tell him their PIN numbers for their bank cards. It was also clear to them that he picked out women at random rather than targeting them specifically. Four women had been brutally murdered in the span of six months, and they were all pointing toward this man. Based on the evidence that suggested the women had opened up their doors to this man, it was clear he was using some sort of disguise. Thus, they nicknamed him The Killer Handyman.

Even though the police knew the murders were connected, they didn't have much to go on. They had some blood samples and a footprint, but none of it pointed to anyone in particular. It wasn't until the murder of Mary Glen that they had some solid evidence.

Chapter Three – The Final Murder

Eight weeks later, on December 14, 1999, in the providence where Anna Yarnold had been murdered, a man approached one of the many large homes of Baie-D'Urfe, Quebec. He wore a working man's clothes. When a woman answered the door, he explained to her he was doing yard work in the neighborhood and wanted to offer his services. The woman consulted with her husband and the two decided not to hire him. She later realized how much of a brush with death she'd had.

The man left her home and traveled down the road, where he came to Mary Glen's home. She lived alone in a waterfront home and was employed as a graphic artist who was described as outgoing and well-known in her community. The same man who claimed to be doing yard work in the area walked up her home later on in the day.

The following morning, a housekeeper arrived at the home to perform her scheduled duties. After she had tried multiple times to attract Mary's attention to open the door, she entered the home and found Mary dead in the living room in a pool of her own blood. The police arrived soon after.

Mary had been beaten, stabbed, and sexually assaulted just as the other two women. She'd been beaten in the face with a blunt object and had been stabbed several times. After the forensic photographer had been finished preserving the scene with photo and video, the biologist was called in again. She performed blood stain analysis and projection to determine how the murder played out.

By studying the blood trail, they were able to put together a sequence of events for the attack. There were no signs of forced entry, suggesting Mary opened the door to her attacker. The attack began in the kitchen, where it was very violent. It moved into the side office where evidence showed Mary had succeeded in escaping several times. There were clumps of hair that had been violently ripped out, suggesting she'd tried to escape.

At the bottom of the stairs, the investigators found her bloody glasses. There were also pieces of hair with blood on them there, too. The murder finally ended in the living room where it was very violent and messy.

Investigators discovered faint footprints in the blood that were different from the one's found at Monique's home. The killer had gone back to the steps from the living room to the kitchen, where there was diluted blood in the sink. It was at this point he either washed his hands or he washed something off in the sink. He'd gone to the second floor where police discovered footprints from the killer on the stairs. He'd searched a few rooms upstairs that looked like bedrooms and had found her purse.

On the second day, they were searching her home, they found a fingerprint. Within twenty-four hours, the police had succeeded in tying the fingerprint to a name. It was difficult to analyze, but through careful comparison, the match was made. The fingerprint belonged to a forty-four-year-old Caucasian man named William Fyfe.

Chapter Four – The Man behind the Murders

William Fyfe was born in Toronto, Canada on February 27, 1955. He was later raised by an aunt for unknown reasons. While there were not any incidents during his childhood, friends later recalled there was something a little off about William. When he became an adult, he began working as a handyman.

There is little known about William's childhood as his mother was uncooperative with the police when they asked, and Fyfe spoke little about his mother and growing up. It is unclear whether negative events during his childhood caused him to become the killer he is, or if it was something else entirely.

When the police ran the fingerprint and came back with a name from Mary Glen's murder, they realized Fyfe had some previous convictions in the 1970's for breaking and entering and theft. Since then, it appeared he worked on and off as a freelance handyman, a job that gave him plenty of access to stranger's homes.

At one point, he was married and had a child, but he was with several women on and off throughout his free years. Most people called him charismatic and it was clear he got along with many. At the time the police were searching for him, his residence was Montreal, but his current whereabouts were unknown. The police struggled with the decision to put out a picture to the public naming him as a suspect because they didn't want to frighten him off, but they also wanted to protect the public.

The board decided to give the police some time before they released the photo to the public. That same day, the police received information from one of his ex-girlfriends. She suspected he was staying at his mother's home outside of Barrie, Ontario. Records were checked and it was clear he owned a vehicle, a blue Ford Ranger. This information as passed onto the Ontario provincial police, who were given the information for his potential whereabouts, as well.

Fyfe's mother lived in an old farmhouse out in the country, well off the road. It was difficult for the police to see the vehicles sitting in her driveway, but they suspected they saw a vehicle that looked similar to William Fyfe's. They backed off and waited in the area for Fyfe to make a mistake. Twenty-four-hour surveillance was set up at his mother's home to keep him from escaping and murdering another person.

Once they had him under surveillance, the police took the investigation public and released the information to the newspapers to drum up witnesses. The good thing about this is that it went national, reaching Fyfe's attention. During the surveillance, Fyfe made some key mistakes that pinpointed him as the murderer.

First, William Fyfe left his mother's home and went to Toronto where he looked for the National Post and other newspapers. Then he put in an order to the Gazette from Montreal in order to keep an eye on himself in the paper. On December 21, 1999, after three days of being home, he was in Barrie driving around. He was watched as he went to a church to drop off some running shoes outside of a bin.

The police quickly retrieved the shoes after Fyfe left the scene. The biologist confirmed spots on the shoes were blood from the victims. On December 22, 1999, the decision was made to arrest William Fyfe. The police followed him to a gas station and waited for him to appear outside. There, they arrested him for the murder of Mary Glen. As he was being arrested, he told one of the police officers:

"Why don't you shoot me now?"

Fyfe was taken to Barrie detachment and was interviewed by several officers. During the interrogation, he chain-smoked and was agitated and upset. He pulled the plug on the camera several times, was arrogant, cold, and threatened to call his lawyer, which he did several times. The police were unable to get much out of him that night, but they had his cigarette butts.

That night, the cigarette butts were sent for analysis, the shoes were sent for testing, and his mother's home and his truck were searched for evidence. On December 22nd, Fyfe was maintaining his innocence but the evidence against his was quickly mounting. The staining on his shoes was confirmed to be human, and there were more traces of blood on his clothing and in his mother's home. The three pairs of shoes he'd dropped off for donation, the hat, napkins, and many other objects were all confirmed to have human blood on them.

The investigators informed Fyfe of the evidence they had against him, and in the weeks that followed, a case against William Fyfe was created. Anna's blood was discovered on a piece of William's clothing at his mother's home. The security footage from Anna's bank showed William Fyfe in it. The bloody footprint on Monique's balcony matched one of the running shoes and the blood droplets were from Fyfe. One of Teresa's stolen rings was found amongst Fyfe's possessions. In the case of Mary Glen, the fingerprint evidence was strengthened by two more discoveries. Another bloody footprint matched the running shoes, and traces of Mary's blood was on Fyfe's clothing.

At the same time, the police were investigating all the other unsolved cases in the area for the previous twenty-five years. They received a phone call from a man named Scattolon who said he'd known Fyfe. They had played hockey together. His mother had been brutally murdered in her home and Fyfe had been inside to paint it. Scattolon wondered if there was a connection.

Almost twenty years had lapsed, yet DNA from the murdered was still available. The DNA matched William Fyfe. Hazel Scattolon was a fifty-two-year-old woman who was stabbed to death and sexually assaulted in 1981. Fyfe pled guilty on September 21, 2001, and faces twenty-five years of prison. The family members were gratified it was over and the cases were closed, but Fyfe hinted to other crimes he might have committed between 1981 and 1999.

There was a time period in the 1980's in the same areas where there was a serial rapist who raped four different women. The first woman was Suzanne Bernier, a woman who lived in Montreal and was fifty-five years old. The second woman was Nicole Raymond, a woman who lived in pointe-Claire and was twenty-six years old. The third woman was Louise Blanc, a thirty-seven-year-old resident of Ste. Adele. The fourth woman was Pauline Laplante, a forty-four-year-old resident of Piedmont.

The police believe William Fyfe was the serial rapist nicknamed The Plumber due to his method of getting into these women's homes. He would wear a plumber's uniform and claim the landlord had sent him to fix a water leak in the women's apartments. Once he was inside, he would brutally rape them.

Fyfe denied involved in Janet Kuchinksy's death. He discussed his crimes in clinical detail, letting the police know he was involved in them, but he was silent when they asked him about his motives.

William Fyfe will get out of prison when he is sixty-nine years old due to Canada having a law that allows criminals to be held for only twenty-five years. However, he has been admitted to a psychiatric hospital and chances look slim he will ever be released. Fyfe still maintains his silence on his childhood and his motives for raping and killing all these women.

If proven to be the rapist and murderer in several other open cases, he will be named Canada's worst serial killer to date. Oddly enough, Fyfe doesn't seem interested in being associated with his wrongdoings in a famous way. He seems content to remain on the sidelines, away from the spotlight, unlike most serial killers.

Conclusion

While there is a lot of media given to the cases involving serial killers, there are not that many who have either been caught or confirmed. Still, the thought of a man who seems innocent enough coming into women's homes while they are alone is enough to frighten the public into thinking about leaving their doors unlocked. Members of the communities of the victims, in this case, will never forget the women who died and how they died. William Fyfe has had an everlasting effect on the people who knew him and those who were close to his murders.

Perhaps, in time, more will be discovered about William's childhood and his motives for his crimes, but until then, we can only speculate what turned a seemingly normal child into a murderous monster.

ROBERT HOWARD

MICHAEL KAI GREEN

In October 2015, a decrepit old man named Robert Howard died of natural causes in his cell. In jail he'd led a solitary existence and spoke rarely; indeed he could have been any criminal counting down his time to release except for the fact he never stood a chance of ever getting out of prison. He was serving a life sentence for murder and simultaneously under investigation for the disappearances of other young girls that he would have had access to during a horrifically brutal life of sexual crime. Robert Howard led a gruesome life of crime, rape, brutality and murder and he called himself The Wolfman.

The name certainly conjures interesting and scary thoughts; The Wolfman sounds like a movie about werewolves or a mythical creature and he actually even gave himself a new middle name, Lesarian, believed to be a mythical child killer. He also called himself the Wolfhill Werewolf and he was certainly beastly enough to be deserving of such a name, even if he was not particularly physically grotesque.

After a criminal career that spanned 40 years, this book will look at the man behind the name, The Wolfman. I want to look at what turned him into the beast he became and why he went to such grotesque lengths with his crimes. I want to look at whether there was more to the man than meets the eye, or whether he was just a psychotic murderer and rapist. I will also look at the public opinion of him and the media interest that followed the heinous crimes committed in his active years.

MURDER FILE: ROBERT 'THE WOLFMAN' HOWARD
THE EARLY YEARS

In 1944, Robert Howard was born in an unassuming part of Southern Ireland, County Laois, in a rural area called Wolfhill. He was taller than his childhood friends and had an awkward manner, but he was bright enough and did reasonably well in his classes. Interviews with school mates at an early age suggested that had no particular disposition to some of the crimes he would go on to commit, even if he skipped compulsory school whenever an opportunity presented itself. He had 8 siblings, an uncompromising mother and his father apparently drunk a great deal of alcohol in the local pubs and taverns. When he wasn't boozing, Howard's father worked in the local brick factory and brought home barely enough for them to survive.

He was already in trouble by the young age of 13 when he was convicted of burglary and sent to a young offender's institution close to his home. Unfortunately this was not the kind of institution that troublesome kids get sent to now with emphasis on rehabilitation and morals. St Joseph's Industrial School was an institution administrated by priests and brothers and the truth about such places has only recently started to emerge. It was an Irish Catholic school and the children were starved and beaten often. Former inmates have revealed the gruelling punishments dished out by the relentless priests who would frequently humiliate the children and beat them until they bled. Names were left at the front gate and each child would be just a number, a drone whose life was often damaged irreparably by the constant beatings and starvation. Talk of sexual harassment, torture and rape has also been mentioned but never proven having been so long ago, however given the record of the Catholic Church in Ireland for covering up such instances it would not take a great stretch of the imagination to guess what might have been happening. Howard later claimed to have been a victim of such sexual abuse and used this in his defence but his crimes were ultimately indefensible. For years he would be subjected to this awful regime of farming turnips and moving rocks whilst being starved and beaten and taught the word of god.

Upon release from the institution he returned to the family home but was soon thrown out on the street by his violent, alcoholic father. Wolfhill had many abandoned coal mines leftover from its mining heyday and 16 year old Robert spent many nights sleeping rough in them. He robbed and stole to sustain himself and possibly developed a bitter and twisted view of the world on those cold, lonely nights. One young boy found that his barn had been slept in and they found a blanket and some empty cans of stolen food. They also found a journal listing criminal fantasies of how Howard wanted to break into women's houses and commit violent deeds to them. This is the first inclination we have that Howard had sexually violent fantasies and wanted to commit crimes, rather than robbing and stealing to survive.

Another local source informed reporters that he was out hunting in the woods when he stumbled upon a local farmer performing sexual acts on the young Howard. This could have been Howard's way of getting money to survive. The man did not get in the way of the pair but shot his shotgun in the air in disgust. Whether he made money by selling himself is not confirmed, although he certainly continued on a criminal spiral, stealing cars and taking goods from shops until he was caught again and sent to another, equally brutal Catholic institution. This particular precursor to prison was equally renowned as a horrific institution with beatings, humiliation and abuse rife amongst the staff and inmates. One priest would later go public in saying that it was extraordinarily violent and the boys usually ended up very disturbed.

MURDER FILE: ROBERT 'THE WOLFMAN' HOWARD THE FIRST CONVICTED SEX ATTACKS

Presumably sick of Irish Catholic institutions, and intent on a life of crime, Howard travelled to England after release from a young offender's institution for the second time. Given the harsh conditions imposed upon him during these brutal periods it would be only logical to assume he was a fairly unstable individual at this point. He continued his life of crime in England and robbed and stole to survive, living rough whenever he could not find a place to stay.

Shortly after his 21st birthday, his crimes escalated into sexual abuse as he broke into a London home and pretended he was a doctor, ordering a young girl to undress. He attempted to rape the 6 year old girl and left violently beat her, almost killing her. He fled the scene after he heard someone coming but he escaped. Strangely, he returned to exactly the same house soon after to try again with the same girl but he got caught. His sentence seems insanely lenient as he received 9 days in borstal, and then as was common at the time, he was deported back to Ireland. The governments of both countries seemed eager to avoid media attention on keeping prisoners of the other nationality, given the troubles north of the border in Ireland, which resulted in the ridiculous 9 day sentence and subsequent deportation and release. Howard had a taste of England and chose not to stay in Ireland for long.

It seems ridiculous that a man caught red handed attempting to rape a 6 year old would have been released after 9 days in borstal, and much investigation was done into why his sentence was so lenient. Much of this centred on the political ramifications of the UK holding Irish nationals as prisoner. Needless to say, this should have been the end of the story as the Irish authorities obviously did not realise the sincerity of the situation and what heinous deeds the man they released would go on to commit.

MURDER FILE: ROBERT 'THE WOLFMAN' HOWARD
CONTINUED LIFE OF CRIME

Upon his return to England, Howard was now an extremely dangerous man intent on a life of crime and sexual assault. In 1969, the same year as the Apollo moon landing, Howard found himself in Durham, and continued on his path of destruction. He broke into a house and attempted to rape a young woman, causing her immense physical injury before she escaped and ran down the road, naked and screaming in a fit of hysterics. In a fit of lustful rage he chased her but neighbours managed to get the better of him and he was promptly arrested. After a very short court session he was sentenced to 6 years imprisonment in Frankland Prison, despite the possible political ramifications. The court heard at this time of the life of crime and the judge decided that a spell in an institution was what was needed. Early release from a jail term is usually reserved for those who demonstrate good behaviour, although Howard's period in adult prison seems to have been filled with fights and bad behaviour, having assaulted a female police officer and beaten her badly before being dragged away. Despite this, or perhaps they just wanted rid of him, Howard was released from Frankland and sent back to Ireland where he did stay for a while.

Documents were much easier to forge in the 1970's and Howard had obviously gotten a false identity as he found a job in County Cork, working on a factory near the coastal town of Youghal. He called himself Lesley Cahill but although he was now employed, he would soon resume a life of crime that he had been following since a young age.

It is very easy to blame the authorities in such cases but it really looks as though something should have been done to at least attempt to evaluate and rehabilitate the Howard before he was released and allowed to go on to commit murder.

MURDER FILE: ROBERT 'THE WOLFMAN' HOWARD
THE NEXT SEX ATTACKS

Now back in Ireland, and with a new name and a new job, Howard, or Cahill as he was calling himself could have gone on to lead a somewhat normal life. It seems though, that he was intent on sexual assault and rape as a preferred career choice and before long, he was up to his old tricks. In May of 1973, Howard broke into yet another house and tried to have his way with a woman of almost 60. The house was next door to the place he'd been staying and he must have done some reconnaissance on her situation as he knew she lived alone. He stole her belongings and beta her up, breaking her ankle as e dragged her around. Her tied her to the bed and repeatedly raped her before driving away in her car. She may have died if some family did not come for a visit the following morning.

Willie Doyle, a local police officer said of the attack:

"She was a very vulnerable person. She might have suffocated, but luckily for her some relations called the next morning and found her. She was very traumatised."

After a short investigation, police concluded that Howard was the perpetrator and a warrant was put out for his arrest. He was found at Dublin airport and the police noted how passive and courteous he seemed, far too polite to be the rapist villain they were looking for. Psychologists who interviewed Howard after the arrest stated that he should have been locked up for a very long time as he was an explosive and unpredictable psychopath. He could have been sentenced to life but instead he received 10 years imprisonment. This time there would be no release for good behaviour, although by all accounts it seems his second term in a HM Prison seems uneventful. He served the majority of his sentence and was released in 1981, where upon he returned to Wolfhill in Ireland and unsurprisingly continued on his life of criminality. This time there would be fatalities, quite how many is still not known to police.

MURDER FILE: ROBERT 'THE WOLFMAN' HOWARD CONTINUED CRIMINALITY

Howard was mentioned in a report from a lady who had previous experience of sexual assault as the media found out about her appalling case of events. She was "the Kilkenny incest victim" and was repeatedly raped by her own sick father. He abused her, beat her, tortured and even impregnated her at the age of 15. She told police after the case emerged that Howard would come over to the house and drink whiskey with her father, sharing gruesome details of Howard's previous rapes and crimes and even boasting of new ones. After the story broke in the newspapers, the girl's father was arrested and sentenced to 7 years in prison. Thankfully, he would never be allowed to see his daughter again.

Somehow, Howard managed to find himself a wife and he married a young woman that he'd met in an Irish hospital. They married couple were awaiting social housing and drifted around the city of Dublin with no fixed abode for some time. Friends of the girl would have described her as vulnerable and deeply fragile, emotionally and physically, and they later told police that she'd told them just how evil and violently abusive Howard could be towards her. They lived a turbulent life together and drifted apart when he was jailed for robbery in 1988. He served another year and a half in prison, his 3rd spell, and travelled north of the border in 1990 to check himself into an alcohol addiction facility in Newry. After the treatment, which was run by nuns and given his personal experiences with the Catholic Church can't have been too successful, he met another woman called Pat Quinn and they moved together to Castlederg in County Tyrone. They registered for public housing but had a long line in front of them and ended up in a caravan site whilst they waited. It was during this wait that another young and vulnerable woman, aged just 22 was awaiting social housing and stayed for a few nights with Howard. According to her testimony, Howard tied her up and kept her prisoner for 3 weeks whilst repeatedly raping her. Family would eventually arrive to take her away but inevitably her life would never be the same after that awful experience. The worst part of this crime was that she got pregnant as a result of the rape but did not tell police until some years later and she was considered too weak to give evidence, and so Howard was never charged with this crime.

MURDER FILE: ROBERT 'THE WOLFMAN' HOWARD PHSYCOLOGICAL PROFILING

When studied and questioned by specialists, Howard reacted very differently to what was expected. Judging from the growing list of awful crimes he had committed, psychologists expected a vile monster that was aggressive and arrogant when spoken to but he was far from that. He was smart and sophisticated, even charming when spoken to and he openly spoke of some of his crimes as though it were normal behaviour. Whether this came from his tormented life of institutions and homelessness remains to be seen but the life of crime he embarked upon sent him into a devastating spiral causing the emotional breakdown of many of his victims who were subjected to rape and vile abuse.

It was an extreme failure on the account of social services and of the authorities who failed to notice the actions and signs of a monster that was without remorse and preyed on vulnerable women of all ages and descriptions; even on children.

During sentencing for another rape charge, Dr Bownes, a psychiatrist working for the prosecution said:

"He has the propensity not only to commit further offences of a similar nature, but also to escalate his offending behaviour."

"He uses a sophisticated grooming process and selects vulnerable victims"

"Howard shows a pattern of behaviour had been established over many years and would be extremely resistant to change".

"I was somewhat surprised by the leniency of the sentence. In retrospect, we can see the system failed disastrously."

Dr Bownes was extremely concerned when the news broke about Howard's conviction and relatively short sentence of 3 years suspended sentence. Bownes had described Howard as a serial offender and if not locked away in an institution with the right facilities to treat his mental illness, he would undoubtedly reoffend and on an even larger scale.

MURDER FILE: ROBERT 'THE WOLFMAN' HOWARD THE BEGINNING OF THE END

In January of 1995, Howard, who must have been quite used to this by now, was in court on a charge of rape. Quite astonishingly, even with the psychiatric reports available, Howard was given a 3 year suspended sentence and told to stay away from younger girls. Quite what sort of message this sent to the public is beyond comprehension but Howard was released and sent home. The judge must have hung his head in shame when he heard the news to come.

Upon release Howard was almost immediately in trouble again, this time not with the law but apparently with a splinter group of the IRA. Some high ranking members found out about Howard's activities and acted to put an end to it. Howard fled to Scotland, where he informed the housing association that he was being hunted and needed a secure residence. 2 months after his suspended sentence started, Glasgow council obliged and he started to live in a rough area of Glasgow, conveniently close to schools. Pat Quinn came and stayed with him whilst he moved for unknown reasons. The ground was shrinking beneath him as the PSNI, or Police Service of Northern Ireland had got their act together and informed Glasgow council about Howard's previous actions, or the criminal record that they knew of. This alone made him the prime suspect of the murder of Arlene Atkinson. He came back and forth from Ireland, but maintained permanent residence in Scotland, and Pat Quinn left him when he found a new, vulnerable girlfriend to prey on. He met the girl in a local pub and she had a 10 year old girl, who he may have also abused at some point.

The media then started to hound him. National papers started to publish pictures of his face and list in great detail his previous convictions and possible crimes. He was linked with almost every unsolved crime in the past 30 years and the public responded violently. A mob formed and gathered at his apartment, baying for blood. Howard escaped and was moved by the police to South London, where he was similarly hounded. He moved again to different locations and social services struggled to keep up with him. In 1999, a year before the millennium, a child protection officer noted that he was living in Kent with a woman called Mary.

MURDER FILE: ROBERT 'THE WOLFMAN' HOWARD
THE END OF THE ROAD

Hannah Williams had lived an unfortunate childhood. Her parents had bitterly gone their separate ways and she herself had been subject to sexual abuse from her mother's boyfriend. She had been admitted to facilities that deal with these issues and they noted she had learning difficulties and behavioural issues. In 2001 she was living in a rundown area of Deptford, South London.

The worst possible thing then happened as she was introduced to Howard, through his girlfriend Mary as Hannah and Mary knew each other well through Hannah's mother. Howard apparently took great interest in her and the mother and Mary must have not known about Howard's past because they cannot have understood what would happen next. Hannah took a little trip to the market, alone, and met her brother who was working there. Deptford was not a particularly prosperous area and she had very little money but she dreamed of buying new clothes and shoes. Kevin, her brother remembered hearing her take a phone call and she said "I'm going now."

Hannah had never run away from home, despite her previous troubles, and her mother started to worry when she didn't come home. She had told her mother previously that she was going to meet a friend but she would never come home from wherever she was. She frantically called the police and they didn't seem to take the report seriously so Bernadette went looking on her own. She recruited friends and fellow community members who would work in shifts, driving around the streets looking for the young girl. She made posters and phoned everybody she possibly could to get any information regarding her whereabouts. Several police officers were dismissed after the investigation for not taking enough care and due diligence in the initial stages of the investigation, and with good reason. The media published her pictures and launched campaigns but she was not found and her mother was understandably heartbroken. Her body would not be found for another year.

Workers were clearing a piece of land to make way for a new flyover as part of the Channel Tunnel development when they uncovered something in the undergrowth. Almost a year after the disappearance, a machine used for clearing large pieces of dirt uncovered the decomposing body of a young girl. She had been wrapped in blue plastic and police initially thought it had been another missing girl until the matched the clothes to those Hannah had been wearing on the day she went missing. Police informed Bernadette of the discovery, but she had already seen what was going on via the news on television and she was distraught.

"I finally found out my daughter was dead, and that her body had been found, by watching it on the telly. To find out that way was unforgivable. I screamed and then I cried and cried."

"She would have made a beautiful bride, but instead of a white wedding, we had a white funeral."

Police examined the decomposing remains and did not take long to draw a list of suspects. Top of the list was Robert Howard and the giveaway had been that he'd used his girlfriend Mary's mobile phone to call her just before she died. She'd been raped and strangled in the most horrific way and the rope was still around the neck of the body when it was found. Howard was arrested in March 2002 and would not leave prison for the remainder of his life.

The trial was set for the following year and although they had no forensic evidence of Howard's involvement, they had circumstantial evidence as his whereabouts could not be proven at the time of her disappearance and the long line of character witnesses that wanted to put Howard away for the rest of his life. A young girl even came to court to tell the judge that Howard had tried to take her to exactly the same place where the murder had happened and assault her but she'd escaped.

Gradually, victims from the past bravely came forward and gave grizzly details from their ordeals at the man who called himself The Wolfman. Previous victims told of the particular methods that Howard used in his attacks, namely with the rope around the neck which happened to be the link they needed. In 3 short hours, the jury finished their verdict and were obviously sickened by the offences Howard had committed as they gave a guilty verdict and sent him for sentencing.

MURDER FILE: ROBERT 'THE WOLFMAN' HOWARD
SENTENCING

The judge delivered a damning verdict of the authorities who'd let him go with lenient sentences in the past and held nothing back when delivering his verdict. Mr Justice McKinnon, the judge presiding over the case said that he had no regrets about handing Howard a life sentence and that he only wished it had been done sooner.

"It is clear that you are a danger to teenage girls and other women, and have been for a very long time."

Howard, though now serving a life sentence was also still under investigation for the murder of Arlene Atkinson, and the media were restricted on what they could publish. When the verdict of life was given, the families rejoiced as they felt they could finally start to grieve as the monster had been put away for the rest of his life. Surprisingly, Howard was acquitted of the murder of Arlene in Belfast because previous evidence could not be introduced into the court. There was a furious uproar from the public who noted the flaws of the legal system and felt Arlene deserved more justice than that. In the United States, Howard would have faced the death penalty. The jury were aware of the criminal history of Robert Howard but they were not allowed to use this as evidence.

Since the sentencing and whilst in prison, Howard cut a lonely figure and psychologists tried to study his behaviour. It seemed as though he was resigned to spending his remaining days in relative peace behind the prison walls and he kept to himself whilst the media tried to pin every crime in the unsolved case book on him. It would not surprise many to find him guilty of at least a few of those crimes and a taskforce was set up amongst investigators collaborating from Northern Ireland, Ireland and the United Kingdom. Inquiries were also set up to deal with the handling of Howard and his early releases for which there was still no explanation. He was allowed freedom when he should have had none for the earlier crimes he committed and the public were rightfully outraged.

MURDER FILE: ROBERT 'THE WOLFMAN' HOWARD AFTERMATH

Robert Howard was the subject of much debate and media attention after the full details of his brutal past came to light. The spotlight shined on the legal system and specifically dealings and failures made between deals between the governments of the United Kingdom and Ireland. These failures let a clearly psychotic rapist loose, and allowed him to murder one girl, probably 2 and possible more.

A journalist wrote a book about missing Women from Ireland and has linked Howard to many disappearances over the periods of time he was out of jail. He stressed the importance of further investigations,

"This was a man who travelled freely all over Ireland and the UK, and lived in many places. The police should be looking at all unsolved disappearances, murders and sex crimes against women and girls during the periods when he was at large. They should be asking, 'Where was Howard?' "

As a direct result of Robert Howard, Ireland set up a sexual offenders register in 2001, many years after it should have and liaison between the police forces of all nations involved have improved when it comes to searching for dangerous suspects. The monitoring of sex offenders' on the lists in all nations involved has also improved and anonymous phone lines have been set up for victims of any sexual attacks.

The family of Hannah got closure after the trial and they would not have been sad to hear the news of his passing. His death, although he suffered in jail for some time, would have been bittersweet as young Hannah would have grown into a beautiful woman but she now would never have the opportunity. It was equally sad for the parents of Arlene Atkinson, whose parents knew the killer of their daughter, but he was never punished for the crime.

MURDER FILE: ROBERT 'THE WOLFMAN' HOWARD
SUMMARY

Robert 'The Wolfman' Howard was a sick and twisted killer. He was also a skilled one that targeted vulnerable children and meticulously and ruthlessly preyed upon them. He groomed girls into thinking he was a safe person to be with and he played the system. He tracked down marginalised, vulnerable women to use as cover and seduced them into thinking he was harmless.

From a young age Howard was failed by the system. At first he was failed by the Catholic institutions for young offenders where he was beaten, starved and manipulated beyond comprehension. Only recently have these institutions been found out and closed down for good. He was also failed by his family during childhood, where he was thrown out and forced to fend for himself. The troubles in the institutions, followed by the awful upbringing and living rough meant he was not of a sound mind from an early age and the failures continued.

He was failed by the justice system of both Ireland and the UK, who failed to spot the risks he posed to the public and he was not given the correct rehabilitation and support as his crimes grew in violence and stature. In this respect the public were also failed as the justice system did not protect the scores of victims from the evil man. It was quite clear from reading the long list of crimes he committed, even before he murdered that he should not have been allowed to roam the streets as he stole and raped his way through 4 different countries. The security forces of these countries failed to keep tabs on him and monitor his life of crime.

So the life of the Wolfman would appear to be a life full of failures. He was clearly psychotic and possibly schizophrenic given the reaction of the Irish police force when the arrested him and said he seemed like a nice man. He was indeed a charming fellow, but also a brutal murderer that preyed on children and women and had a brutal past. He was of no use to anyone. Perhaps the only good thing to come from researching about this person is the fact that Ireland set up a sex offenders' list, practically as a result of his actions and support for victims of this crime grew. Liaison between police forces also developed to catch future sex attackers that try to evade the law by moving around. It does not make for good reading, researching the life of this person and not a nice a word has been mentioned about him. I feel deep sympathy for the victims' families and to the victims of his ruthless sex attacks. His was a life dedicated to crime and it was allowed to continue for a great deal longer than it should have. Let us hope that the lessons have been learned on all sides of this story and someone like Robert Howard is never allowed to do anything similar ever again.

A MONSTER IN THE CHURCH

PAULA HEARST

CHAPTER ONE

It was a cold winter night in November when the Hansen family attended a service at the Jehovah Lutheran Church in St.Paul, Minnesota. It was a "family night" at the church. Ellen Hansen and her two daughters, Cassie and Vanessa had looked forward to the evening at the church. There would be interactive games and stories plus the young girls would be able to see their friends.

Bill, the girl's father, had other business to attend to that night. He watched as his young daughters got into the car with his wife.

"It is etched in my memory," Bill Hansen recalled. "We had supper and the girls got in the car. Ellen was driving. And they were in the garage and Cassie was sitting in the passenger seat. And she (Cassie) was blowing kisses at me through the window. Waving goodbye."

Ellen arrived at the church at around 6:40 p.m for the 7:00 service. They liked to arrive early and socialize with the other church members before the sermon began. The girls proceeded to go to the children's area, located on the lower level of the church. It was their designated place to be as they usually had their Sunday School classes there, they called it the "Kid's Kingdom."

"I have to go to the bathroom," Cassie said to her mother at around 6:50 p.m.

"Okay," Ellen said. "You know where it's at?"

"I'll be right back," Cassie nodded her head.

Ellen watched her daughter leave and returned her attention to Vanessa and her other playmates. A few minutes later, however, Ellen realized that Cassie had not returned to the auditorium area and began to search for her daughter.

"Cassie?" Ellen called out.

She passed the rest of congregants milling into the auditorium. Her eyes scanning for her daughter among the clusters of families filing into the church.

"Cassie!"

"What's wrong?" one of the church staff members asked.

"I can't find my daughter," Ellen said.

The two began searching for the little girl, poking their head in the bathroom stalls and then going through every nook and cranny of the church.

"She's wearing a blue dress," Ellen said, trying to collect her thoughts. "She's blonde. Blue dress. Blue skirt. White blouse.

It started as a casual search. Cassie had probably went somewhere inside the church, got distracted and lost track of time.

"There you are!" would be the words everyone expected to hear.

As the minutes went by, however, this casual search soon turned into full blown panic. All of the staff members and congregants now began searching through the church, going upstairs and down.

"Cassie!"

Her heart pounding out of her chest, Ellen called her husband.

"I got the phone call from Ellen," Bill said. "Saying that Cassie was missing. And my heart stopped and I think I was breathing heavy, you know, just thinking 'oh boy,' because you know your child and you know that she would just not walk away from something like that. Right away, I know something was definitely wrong."

Ellen and the congregation looked throughout the church for Cassie to no avail.

The police arrived and the response was immediate. Cassie's photograph was promptly distributed to every news outlet and street flyers were made on the spot.

The search began and lasted all night.

"We stayed up all night," Ellen said. "People came all night long to help. There were a couple hundred people. Helping us search."

Police did door to door search in the neighborhood, inquiring with folks with a picture of Cassie. Church and neighborhood volunteers rallied right away and a command center was set up at the church.

There was no sign of Cassie.

She had disappeared into thin air.

CHAPTER TWO

The next morning at 11 o'clock, the police found Cassie's body

"Oh no!" one of the congregants screamed as the word was given to the people who had gathered in the church.

"The search has been called off," the officer in charge said solemnly.

In a dumpster, behind an auto repair shop that was three miles from the church, the body of Cassie Hansen had been found.

The members of the church wailed in agony. Some people stood in shock, frozen in grief.

Things like this don't happen here.

"It truly incensed the community," one of the officers on the scene said. "It incensed a lot of police officers. It was as if he seemed to be treating her as a piece of trash."

One of Cassie's leather shoes without the buckles were found a few blocks away from the dumpster while her second shoe was found later nearby.

"The idea of a church is one place you can go and you'd let your daughter go to a restroom," Catherine Lowe, crime reporter said. "That's something you would do. You'd feel a safeness, there are good people all in there together the last thing you would ever expect, and you'd have no reason to expect a stranger to come into a church and abduct a child."

The autopsy on Cassie's body would reveal no sexual penetration but that some type of sexual act had taken place.

Semen found on her dress would reveal that the perpetrator had type O blood. They would also find unusual, foreign hairs.

Cassie had been strangled to death by a two and a half inch belt, the time of death occurring between 8 o'clock and midnight. The young girl had abrasions on her body which indicated that another belt was used to restrain her. The child had been punched in her face, head, ribs and shoulder. She had scratches on her face that were consistent with someone's hand being held over her mouth.

The police did have one vague description of a possible suspect, however.

One of the church congregants reported seeing a Caucasian male, about 50-60 years old, enter the bathroom area on the night of Cassie's disappearance. He had white hair and glasses.

Who was he?

Police went to work, digging up information on any and all sex offenders in the area.

"We had a total of 107 people who had been identified by the community," an officer said. "Or through police investigation of being possible suspects. Of those 107 individuals, 57 of them either lived or worked in the area where the little girl was abducted from."

Police would rounded up these past offenders and the interrogations began.

They quickly got a suspect and then a confession.

From a crazy woman.

"Vondell Quanley," Thomas Poch said. "A woman from Texas who had claimed to have killed Cassie Hansen. And when she came to the attention of St. Paul police and allegedly made a confession it turned out that what she did was read details in the paper and then recite them. She said 'I claim I acted alone.' Well, it was quite obvious that she couldn't generate seminal fluid and that this was a sham and a fraud."

A helpful call did come in, however. Two witnesses claim that they saw an older white male carrying a motionless child near the auto body shop dumpster on the night Cassie disappeared.

Police followed up on this lead as it echoed what the church congregant witnessed near the church bathrooms.

An elderly white man. White hair. Glasses.

Needing more to go on, the St. Paul police contacted the FBI unit.

With their assistance, the FBI helped St. Paul police come up with a behavioral profile of the child murderer.

"The killer is most likely a Caucasian male," the FBI profiler said. "Someone who is considered a loner."

"How do you mean?"

"We're not talking about someone who is the life of the party here. He can blend in. He can be invisible."

"So the people in church wouldn't necessarily notice him right off the bat?"

"Precisely," the profiler said. "This is a guy who doesn't think a whole lot of himself and automatically thinks that everyone around him sees him the same way. No value. So he keeps to himself and lashes out when he can. He probably has a low-level job or is unemployed.

Probably has had numerous sex offenses in the past. He likes to frequent parks or schoolyards. You know, the creepy guy standing on the periphery. He's a voyeur. He watches his victims from afar before making his move. He trolls around at night, thinking of himself as some kind of predator. He can hide better at night. It brings out his mood, his compulsion."

"Do you think he's still here?"

"That's the illogical thing. The perp will not leave the area. He is limited in funds and can't move around easy. He feels put upon and justified in his actions. That he's entitled to whatever he wants. So he often takes a souvenir from his victims. A lock of hair. An article of clothing. Anything that marks the moment. His moment of triumph. He may also return to the scene of the crime, feeling the need to talk about it with someone."

CHAPTER THREE

The perp in the case of Cassie Hansen, did just that courtesy of Dorothy Noga.

Noga, a masseuse at the Comfort Center in St. Paul, called in a tip for the police when she became suspicious of one of her clients.

One of her customers, a cab driver named Stuart Knowlton, had been in her massage parlor the day after Cassie's murder.

Noga remembered Knowlton coming into her parlor at 3 a.m in the morning to introduce himself to the staff. He was hunched over, breathing heavy and talked really fast as if he had just been in a sprint.

He handed out business cards to everyone and received a massage from Noga.

"How's that feel?" Noga asked as she kneaded Knowlton's back.

"Great," Stuart said. "But I need a favor."

"What's that?" Noga asked, expecting the usual request for a "special" massage.

"If anyone asks, tell them I was in here last night."

That made Noga suspicious, knowing that Cassie had been murdered the night before.

Stuart Knowlton looked suspicious and fit the profile. He was Caucasian and 56 years old. Single, he worked a low-level job as a taxi driver. He had beady blue eyes set behind thick-set glasses.

Eyes that gave off the thousand yard stare that only a true psychopath can pull off.

He 'looked' the part. But was he the guy?

"I have no urge for any little girls," Knowlton said during police questioning. "I feel sorry for the little girl for her family. But I did not kill her. I didn't even know she was missing until.."

"Is it possible you killed her and forgot?"

"No sir," Knowlton said. "I did not kill her."

"Where were you on the night of the murder?"

"I was on duty driving my taxi cab. Could not have been me."

Noga followed up with police and offered to tape record her conversations with Knowlton.

Police, however, declined her offer as it would have been too dangerous for the masseuse.

The police also did not want to be seen as obtaining information illegally after Knowlton had contacted a lawyer and the lawyer had told him not to talk. Noga decided to override the police order, however. She was a good listener and could always get men to open up to her. She had four kids of her own and wanted to make the safe streets for other families.

She would then have daily phone conversations with Knowlton with same lasting deep into the night. She described him as being "lonely" and that he could not stop talking about Cassie Hansen's murder.

Noga knew that he was the man who did it.

On one occasion, Noga had taken Knowlton out for a drive. They drove past Cassie's church and noticed that Knowlton had become very agitated and wanted to leave.

The nightly phone calls soon became very taxing. Knowlton believed that the two had some kind of romantic connection. Noga was soon putting herself into a corner that she couldn't escape from.

"I would get so depressed talking to him," Noga told the St. Paul Dispatch. "I wanted to give up. I would just sit and cry."

But finally he broke.

Stuart Knowlton confessed to killing Cassie Hansen.

Noga then started taping their conversations and gave the police the tapes. The police encouraged her to keep up the conversations but Knowlton never mentioned his involvement with the murder again. He still talked about the case in a roundabout way but never confessed to the killing again.

The police would catch another break in the case as another person familiar with Knowlton came forward.

Her name was Janice Rettman. She was in charge of St. Paul's Public Housing Office and met Knowlton when he complained that he was about to be evicted from a Roosevelt Homes public housing project. He stated that his wife was leaving him and taking their two children. The welfare payments and food stamps they had been cut off and he had just begun driving a cab. Rettman investigated his claims, however, and discovered that those were not the reasons he was being evicted.

Residents had complained made sexual advances toward young girls in the housing unit.

Knowlton had let two fourteen year old girls into his apartment to play cards. Once inside, he began describing to them where babies came from and began talking about sex, birth control and menstruation. He then asked if they wanted to see his penis. The girls reported the incident to police which then informed the public housing office.

Knowlton was then given a warning by the office that if such an incident would occur again he would be evicted.

Knowlton wouldn't heed the warning. He confronted a nine year old girl and told her to take her pants off for him. The girl was so traumatized that she had recurring nightmares of Knowlton.

Knowlton's wife and children were taken to a women's shelter while he lived in an efficiency apartment. He then told Rettman of his sexual preference for children. He revealed he had spent time in a mental hospital in Traverse City, Michigan after he molested a seven year old girl. He alleged that his own father routinely beat and abused him. And he would talk about shoes a lot.

"I can't remember anyone being as chilling as he was," Rettman recalled as she knew that Knowlton frequented the area where Cassie was murdered. As a cab driver, he would be familiar with the ins and outs of the streets there, the back streets and alleys.

She would call to double-check on his housing situation and found him upset and unwilling to talk. He hung up on her but called her back a few days later. Knowlton said that he "was going through hell, was very lonely, and needed someone to talk to and to visit him."

Rettman offered her services to police, stating that she could meet with Knowlton and wear a wire.

Police accepted her offer.

Knowlton would tell Rettman about the child molestation charges from the Roosevelt Homes, his problems with his wife and his inability to hold down a job. He talked about how he converted to Christianity the previous year after being inspired by a Johnny Cash song.

Knowlton would also make reference to his "explosive temper" during their conversation and mistakenly call Rettman "Dorothy" on two occasions.

"Have you been following the news about Cassie Hansen?" Rettman asked.

"Yeah, I have," Knowlton said. "Police came and talked to me about it."

"Really?"

"They want to find out if he and I were together. If he were up there at the time of the Hansen's girls beatings. I don't even remember where I was that night."

The police then knew they had incriminating evidence against Knowlton. The fact that Cassie had been beaten up had not been released to the public.

"That was crucial and that was very critical," Thomas Poch, prosecuting attorney said. "Because no one had revealed to the press, to the media, to anyone, that she'd been beaten. And only the killer could have known that. Meanwhile, we didn't have any witnesses. It was entirely a circumstantial case."

CHAPTER FOUR

Police followed through with Knowlton's claim that he was working on the night that Cassie Hansen was murdered. With the cooperation of the taxi company, they realized that Knowlton had not turned in his log book. The log book was the time and location of all of a taxi driver's pick-ups and drop-offs.

"What happened to your log book?" police asked Knowlton in another interview.

"It was stolen," Knowlton said.

Knowlton's dispatcher, Donald Whalen would state that he tried to radio Knowlton several times during the night of Cassie's disappearance and could not reach him. Knowlton then tried to buy blank trip sheets from a competing cab company on the day Cassie's body was found.

Dorothy Noga decided to ignore police warnings that Knowlton was dangerous. With her poofy brown hair and overly applied black eye-liner, Noga did not fit the profile of a police informant. She did, however, prove to answer the hero's call when needed.

Noga called Knowlton again in the hopes of entrapping him into making incriminating statements.

"So have you been following the news about Cassie?" Noga asked. "The little girl that was murdered."

"She was a hero for us," one of the police officers said. "She told us that during one of these conversations that he admitted to her that he had killed the little girl. That he had, in effect, killed Cassie. Dorothy Noga agreed and wanted to help in the case and stated that she would be willing to talk to him and to tape these conversations. And she did this hours on end."

Knowlton, however, would not repeat what he told Noga on the phone during their earlier conversation.

Noga didn't realize how much danger she had exposed herself to. After getting off the phone with Knowlton, she was about to close her massage parlor that evening and was confronted by a man inside.

The attack was swift. She left up her hands in defense but the knife slashed through. She squirmed to get away but her assailant stabbed her in the back then slashed down her throat.

Noga crumpled to the ground, losing consciousness as she bled out.

Her assailant escaped into the darkness, blood dripping from his knife.

The thirty-two year old Noga was discovered in the parlor and rushed to the hospital.

"I proceeded to the hospital," one of the policemen on duty said. "Her throat had been slit. Her blood pressure was down to zero. They were certain she was going to die."

Noga would recover from her attack, however. She had been slashed in her throat, back and wrist right after she attempted to record Knowlton's confession.

But Noga had no recollection of the attack. She had to be placed under hypnosis in order to remember the specific details.

During hypnosis, Dorothy was able to remember who stabbed her that night.

She remembered the man's face in the darkness.

It was Stuart Knowlton.

"He jammed a knife straight on in my neck," Noga recalled in a television interview. "Then he pulled it out. Then I knew that he had cut me and I turned my head and he said 'I'll teach you not to talk' and he cut it and he slit it (her throat) all the way down."

She remembered that Stuart had confronted her and accused her of going to the police. He then confessed to the crime, giving her all of the specific details. After he confessed, he took out a knife and began chasing her around the sauna until he slashed at her throat and she lost consciousness.

CHAPTER FIVE

Minnesota State law permits testimony obtained from hypnosis, so any testimony from Noga would have been deemed inadmissible.

The police then focused on the science of the crime.

They had a semen sample that was Type O. DNA was still a long way away from acceptance back in the early 1980s but Stuart Knowlton had Type O blood. The police then acquired a hair sample from Knowlton, sending that along with Cassie Hansen's clothing to the FBI forensic laboratory.

The techs then scraped off any loose hairs and fibers from Cassie's clothing. They wanted to match Knowlton's hair sample with anything on Cassie's clothing.

"Hair comparisons are not a means of absolute personal identification," FBI Lab expert Al Robillard said. "Because a hair matches an individual or has the same microscopic characteristics as that individual's hairs, does not absolutely mean that it came from him. The reason for that is hairs are not so unique that they allow you to reach an absolute conclusion. Its possible that two hairs are so alike that they can't be distinguished microscopically could come from two separate individuals."

But Robillard would make a hair discovery on Cassie's dress that he had never seen before.

"What's so unusual in my career, looking at hairs at the FBI laboratory, I have never seen or I have never matched a hair that had this unusual characteristic. A hair disease called pili annulati. Commonly that is referred to as either ringed hair or banded hair. So I thought this was rather significant."

"If you think of looking at a racoon's tail, you actually see bands. And these bands are created because there is a breakdown in that area of the cuticle that begins to separate."

Robillard then took samples of Knowlton's hair and matched from the ones on Cassie's dress. They both had the same condition.

Pili annulati.

"No doubt about it," Robillard said looking back. "Thousands of hairs over the course of my career. I was only to put two hairs, associate a victim to a suspect, not only through the microscopic characteristics but also through a disease of the hair."

The hair was enough to arrest Knowlton for Cassie's murder.

But asthe police were closing in on Knowlton, the taxi cab driver suffered an accident.

He was crossing the street in St. Paul when a motorist ran into him. The suspect was transported to the hospital where surgeons had to amputate his left leg below the knee.

"It just seemed to me that divine intervention was there," one of the police officers said. "And that the children were going to be protected and that he would not be able to grab another child."

CHAPTER SIX

Noga would take the stand during Knowlton's trial and tell jurors of the telephone call before he attacked her.

"He said he was driving his taxi cab in the vicinity of the Jehovah Evangelical Lutheran church when he needed to use the bathroom," Noga said. "It was there I saw Cassie Hansen."

Knowlton then described greeting Cassie outside the bathroom, talking to her about the church services.

"Would you like to play a game?" he asked.

The girl nodded but remained unsure.

Knowlton lured her outside. Cassie began to cry.

He then her into his cab and molested her.

The little girl kept crying so he put his hand over her mouth until she stopped breathing.

He would then take off both of her shoes before placing her into the dumpster. Knowlton had removed the buckle from the shoe and kept it as a souvenir before dumping the shoes in two separate locations.

"Stuart had a shoe fetish," Janice Rettman said. "When he talked about shoes at first, it meant nothing to me. In retrospect, it was probably more significant than I thought."

The unique hair found on Cassie's hair clothing that matched Stuart Knowlton's own hair strand was enough to convince the jury to find him guilty of first degree murder and second degree misconduct.

He was sentenced to life in prison.

"The evidence from the FBI laboratory was absolutely critical and one piece of evidence that was absolutely essential to tying him in and being able to get a conviction of Stuart Knowlton."

Knowlton was given an opportunity to speak after his sentencing and he went on an incoherent ten minute rant.

"As God is my witness," Knowlton rambled on "I swear to you this day, I did not abduct Cassandra Lynn Hansen from the church she was attending. I had no reason to take anyone's life for God had not given me that right. I have had no reason to have any vengeance against Cassandra Lynn Hansen or Dorothy Noga."

Knowlton would die in prison in 2006 after being denied parole in 2001.

After his sentencing, the Hansen family started a foundation called "Save Cassie's Friends." Two hundred books were printed out in Cassie's honor, raising awareness of child abduction.

SERIAL KILLER GRANDPARENTS : THE TRUE STORY OF RAY & FAYE COPELAND

OLIVIA WATSON

Chapter One

Ray and Faye Copeland are often known as the oldest couple ever to be sentenced to death in the United States. At the ages of 76 and 69, the couple was sentenced to death in separate trials for the murders of five vagrant men that they had taken in, hired, forced to commit fraud, and then finally killed to keep quiet.

While Ray's guilt in the crime was indisputable, Faye's role in the crimes is muddled as she was the victim of severe physical abuse at the hands of Ray. Was she truly involved in the crime? Or was she simply a victim herself?

Ray Copeland was born in Oklahoma in 1914. He had a tough childhood—his family was struggling to survive the Depression and moved around a lot. To help support his family, Ray began a life of petty crime as a young man. He would forge cheques and steal livestock every chance he could.

In the late 1930's, this life of crime caught up to Copeland and he was arrested and sentenced to a year-long jail sentence. After his release in 1940, he met Faye Wilson, a young woman who belonged to a simple family. The two connected and Ray won Faye's heart by promising to always protecting her.

Ray and Faye married only a few months after first meeting. They decided to move from Oklahoma to Missouri and Ray quickly found them a property on the outskirts of the small town of Mooresville. The property was a small plot of farmland that had a simple farmhouse and a few barns, but lots of space for bringing up cattle.

Ray had spent his whole life taking care of cattle, and was convinced that raising and selling cattle would be his fast track path to building a proper life for himself and his family. Ray and Faye had several children in quick succession, which meant that they needed money fast. It wouldn't be long until Ray returned to his old ways, and began to use crime as a means for obtaining money.

Chapter Two

In the late 1980's cattle auction houses throughout the state of Missouri were frequently being swindled. Buyers would show up, make their purchase, pay by cheque and then disappear. The cheques were inevitably worthless.

To combat this problem, cattle auctions in the area began to keep track of buyers who were known to not be good for their money, and they shared these names with other cattle auction houses. If you were blacklisted by one auction house, you would be blacklisted at all the others in the area as well.

Ray Copeland quickly made it onto the cattle auction blacklists. After returning to a life of crime, he quickly built up an increasingly bad reputation. This caused a lot of problems—his whole livelihood was raising cattle and now he couldn't purchase any cattle to raise unless he paid in cold hard cash, something he didn't often have.

Faced with the realization that he could no longer buy cattle himself, he lacked the means to move his family to a new area, and that he was tired of wasting time in jail, he came up with a new plan: a way to use his illegal money-making methods that would allow him to remain undetected.

Ray Copeland began to hire vagrant men from the area to go to cattle auctions with him. He would have the men bid and pay for cattle using his own bad cheques and then sell the cattle before the auction houses realized the cheques bounced. This way, if the auction houses came after someone in relation to the bad cheques, the vagrant men would be responsible, not Ray Copeland.

This scheme worked for Copeland for quite a while. It confused a lot of auction houses and the local police forces for quite some time. As Leland O'Dell, a former sheriff from rural Missouri explained: "It was so odd that so many of them would have cheques but when we went to go look for them, we couldn't find them. We would enter them into the computer, but they never showed up."

Copeland's scheme was smart. No one would expect a man with cheques to be vagrants, and most vagrant men were incredibly difficult to track down.

Eventually, this scheme caught up to Copeland. After police were able to find and interview some of the vagrant men they found out that they had almost all been hired by Ray Copeland. Ray was arrested for his involvement and spent his later incarceration determining how he could further improve this plot.

A while after Ray had been released from jail, the instances of successful cattle fraud scams occurring began to rise again. This time though, all the buyers were repeat customers of the auction houses and none of them could be traced down to be questioned. The only thing that connected them was that at some point in time, many of the buyers had all worked on the same farm owned by 78-year-old Ray Copeland and his wife Faye.

But who exactly were Ray and Faye Copeland, and why had so many of their previous employees seemingly disappeared without a trace?

The answer to this would shock police and Missouri's rural community to their very cores.

Chapter Three

To most, the Copeland's were a regular family living a simple life on their small farm. They appeared to be just a regular elderly farm couple that was a bit shy. They didn't like to socialize with a lot of other people, but that was never really a problem. They seemed completely ordinary.

The Copelands had a difficult life though. Their small farm wasn't enough to support the family so Faye took jobs in local factories and worked as a maid in local motels. When asked why she stood with her husband through all of this difficulty, Faye Copeland simply answered, "Because he was my husband. I was taught from childhood that when you married someone, you stayed with them. The husband was the boss. Ray was always the boss."

The whole family, including Faye, also was required to help out on the farm. They were in way over their heads with the amount of chores and work that needed to be completed everyday, even though none of them earned the family any extra money. Faye would wake up early to go muck out cattle stalls before work.

The family was so poor that when Faye did this, she did it barefoot despite the season. She had one pair of shoes and didn't want them destroyed. She needed them clean to keep up appearances while she spent the rest of her day working her other jobs in town.

When the Copeland children left the farm, Ray looked for farmhands. He was up in age, deaf, and not a great businessman. He was also illiterate. He couldn't read or write which made it difficult for him to keep track of how the business was going. He needed someone to help out with the chores, but also the business side of the ever-struggling farm.

To find these workers, Ray would visit local homeless missions. He would come in and ask people if they would like to go out and make some money and get paid at the end of the day. He would even offer to help the men get set up with bank accounts for their new finances.

These men were almost always vagrants. They were men who were usually on the run, they had addictions, family problems, and mental illness. Most had been arrested for vagrancy or petty theft. Ray Copeland would pay them $50 a day for their labour and would provide them with room and board if the workers wanted to stay on at the farm long-term. For someone who had been previously homeless, a steady paycheque and a place to live in a quiet rural setting would have been paradise. Many jumped at Ray Copeland's offer.

One of the men who went to live and work on the Copeland's farm was 27-year-old Dennis Murphy. Murphy was a drifter from Illinois who was down on his luck when Copeland offered him steady work and a place to live. Murphy was also wanted in connection to writing bad cheques to cattle auction houses.

In 1986, a sheriff's deputy following up on Murphy's several instances of fraud visited the Copeland farm after hearing from other vagrant men that he had gone there to work and hadn't been seen since. The deputy asked Copeland if he knew Murphy's recent whereabouts. Copeland replied that the man had simply took off one day, and he hadn't heard from him since.

Copeland claimed that most of the workers he hired would leave in the middle of the night and he would never see them again. Murphy was only one example of this. When Copeland was told that Murphy was a thief, he said he wasn't surprised. He had been swindled too. Copeland also had a cheque from Murphy that had bounced due to insufficient funds.

Unbeknownst to Ray Copeland, seven other men in addition to Murphy were currently being investigated in connection to local cattle auction scams. The police had been having an incredibly difficult time tracking down any of the eight men and were getting close to determining that all eight must have left town immediately after committing their crimes.

One day however, a call from an unlikely informant in Nebraska opened up a whole new path of investigation for the police—a path with a sinister turn. What if none of the men could be found because after committing their own crimes, they all became the victim of a heinous serial killer.

Chapter Four

The unlikely informant from Nebraska was Jack McCormick, a drifter and small time conman who had at one time worked on Ray Copeland's farm. He liked to tell stories and told police that he thought he had seen human remains including a skull on the Copeland's farm during his time there.

Due to the extensive criminal past Copeland had, and the fact that many of the missing men had worked for Copeland as well, police decided to follow up on McCormick's story.

The Copeland's farm covered 40 acres and included a pond, a barn, fields, and woods. A major search was launched on the property by police. They surveyed the area looking for possible burial sites, human remains, or crime scenes. Scent dogs and backhoes were both used in the search which lasted for weeks. Searchers even poked holes in the walls to find any hollow hiding spots.

After nine days of searching without success, police began to doubt McCormick's story so they decided to bring him back to his former employers farm.

Former sheriff O'Dell was one of them men who brought McCormick back to the Copeland's farm. He remembers telling the man just point to where this skull and leg bones were.

When confronted with this, McCormick got nervous. He told police he could've been mistaken. Perhaps he had actually just seen a discarded pan or other large object poking the bushes. He asked to be taken away from the farm right away—he didn't want to spend a minute more than needed to there.

After this frustrating experience, police decided to launch an in-depth investigation into the background of Ray Copeland. What they found showed an interesting coincidence. Twenty years earlier, Copeland had been arrested several times for the same thing his vagrant workers had—writing bad cheques.

Copeland had seemingly calmed down since then, though. It had been over 20 years since he had wound up in jail, and he had never been arrested for a violent crime. Police soon learned that Copeland worked on some other farms in the area to earn extra money.

One such farm was only a few miles from Copeland's own farm. These properties now needed to be searched as well. Although they weren't quite sure how all the pieces fit together yet, police were almost certain that the disappearance of Murphy and the seven other missing vagrant men were somehow connected to Copeland.

When police searched this secondary location, they made a startling discovery in the barn were Copeland worked moving around large bales of hay. In the back corner of the barn, hidden underneath and behind several large hay bales was a shallow grave—in it, were the bodies of three men lined up head-to-toe-to-head. They had probably been in the grave for two or three years, and were now completely unrecognizable due to the amount of decomposition that had taken place.

The bodies were wrapped in blankets, which kept them dry so they had not decomposed down to skeletal remains. To help this, the soil was also clay, which helps to ward of decomposition as well. Instead, the skin of the bodies had dried out and shrivelled like a mummy.

The three men had been killed by single gunshot wounds to the head. But there was no evidence linking Ray Copeland or anyone else to the crimes. A few days later in another barn on the same property police removed hundreds of bales of hay and found another body under a floorboard.

Six weeks later in a nearby well was yet another body. This man had been wearing a belt that read Dennis across the front. But was this Dennis Murphy? And was his killer Ray Copeland?

Chapter Five

After police found the remains of five different men on a farm connected to Ray Copeland, they reinterviewed McCormick. This time, McCormick was more confident in his memories of his former boss.

McCormick told police that Ray Copeland had been running a cheque fraud scam. He said Copeland had given him a few hundred dollars to open a chequing account and told him to list a post office box as his address. He then took McCormick to cattle auctions and sat in the stands, signalling to McCormick when to bid on the cattle.

When he won the bidding, McCormick would pay for the cattle with a cheque. After a couple of his cheques cleared he would be in good standing with the auction house. They next time they returned, he was able to spend more money and write even larger cheques under the pretence that the cheque would be good as well when it was brought to the bank. It almost always bounced the second time.

Copeland would sell the cattle bought under McCormick's name and kept the profits himself. But before the cheque had a chance to bounce, Copeland confronted McCormick with a gun.

Copeland told McCormick that there was a raccoon living in a hole in his barn and he needed the worker's help to get rid of it. He wanted McCormick to crouch down next to the hole and poke the raccoon with a stick while Ray waited with his gun. At this time, McCormick was already nervous around his large, aggressive boss who he knew was orchestrating a fraud scam at the time.

The skittish McCormick bent to Copeland's will and began to crouch down in the barn and poke at the hole with a stick. When nothing happened, Ray told him to keep going. McCormick felt a chill go up his spine and quickly looked back up at his boss to see him pointing his '22 rifle not at the hole where the raccoon was allegedly going to be running out of but directly at his own head.

McCormick promised Ray he would leave the area and never come back if he spared his life. Ray agreed, and McCormick immediately left Missouri behind him. For five months the vagrant man was quiet about his ordeal, and Ray's scam plot, as he still feared Copeland. He knew his former boss had no problems taking lives, so he did what he felt he needed to do to protect his.

When Police searched the Copeland's home, they found a '22 rifle and an assortment of men's clothing, none of which belonged to Ray. They also found several pairs of men's shoes in a range of sizes, none of which fit Ray or their sons, and a bunch of empty suitcases.

Most damningly though, hidden in a camera case was a list of names. The list was a record of men who had worked for Ray Copeland in the past. Next to four of the names was an X, which corresponded with four vagrant men who were wanted in connection to bad cheques that had been given to pay for cattle at nearby auctions. One of which, was Dennis Murphy.

Four names were marked with an X on Copeland's list, and five bodies had been found hidden around a farm Copeland had worked on. It was obvious to investigators that they needed to find a way to have the four bodies positively identified as soon as possible.

Chapter Six

Investigators working on the Copeland case sent the skulls of the five bodies to a forensic odontologist who photographed and x-rayed each of the skulls to compare the dental markings to dental charts from each of the men whose names had been marked with an X. Although this is a common practice in the world of forensic science and criminal investigation, this instance proved difficult.

All the men on Copeland's list were vagrant and homeless. While they all had dental records on file from their childhoods, they were now extremely out-of-date. None of the men had received recent dental care. Without recent records, and with a lifetime worth of damage due to improper care, it was difficult to determine whether the dental records didn't match the skulls because they weren't the same people, or if they didn't match any more because of the outdated records.

One of the skulls, however, was easily matched to previous records because of irregularities in the bones around the teeth. This skull had been from the body found in the well on the farm, and it was positively identified as being Dennis Murphy.

Eventually, the four other skulls were able to be positively identified. Three of the four had been names marked with an X on Ray Copeland's list.

The five bodies were sent to Coroner Scott Lindley to be autopsied. In each case, the cause of death was found to be from gunshots fired from a close distance.

"If the shot is fired from close range, the inside of the skull tends to break or flake away and there is more small fractures and damage done to the skull altogether," Lindley has explained.

Inside each of the skulls Lindley also found bullets and bullet fragments. Markings on the bullets were later conclusively determined to have been able to come from only one gun—Ray Copeland's '22 caliber rifle.

Faced with this information, police confidently arrested Ray Copeland for the five men's murders. In a move that shocked many, they also arrested Ray's wife Faye, who they believed had been his accomplice.

But what role exactly did 68-year-old Faye Copeland play in the murders?

Chapter Seven

Faye Copeland claimed she knew nothing about Ray's crimes. She knew about his previous convictions for fraud, of course, but had no idea that Ray had been murdering their employees in a more modern cattle fraud scheme. According to Faye, when the workers disappeared Ray told her that they had simply run off or that he had fired them and they left right away. She had no reason to doubt her husband's stories, the men were vagrants after all, and Ray had emotionally and physically abused Faye their entire marriage so she wasn't about to question him for details.

While in prison, Faye wrote a letter to her husband assuring him that things would calm down soon. While it was meant to be a calming gesture to the man she was married to, Faye's letter was taken by police and used as a known handwriting sample to be compared to the list of names found in the Copeland's home. Faye's handwriting matched the list of the missing men.

While police saw this as damning evidence Faye maintained her insistence that she had no idea about the murders. She explained to police that Ray was illiterate so he often got her to write lists and notes for him all the time. She never asked any questions, it wouldn't have done her any good. When Ray felt like she was questioning his thoughts or choices he simply slapped her across the house to get her to stop.

No one outside of the family had any indication that Ray may have been abusing his wife, but Ray and Faye's children could recall thousands of times Ray lost his temper and took it out on his wife or his children. Al Copeland, one of Ray and Faye's sons, once recalled to police a time when Ray smacked Al's younger brother with a frying pan because he had been scraping the last few mouthfuls of oatmeal out of his bowl with a spoon and Ray didn't like the noise.

Violence had been an everyday occurrence in the Copeland household.

Ray and Faye Copeland were tried in court separately. Prosecutors believed that Ray had acted alone in orchestrating the fraud schemes, including murdering the men afterwards to keep them quiet, but that Faye had known what was going on the whole time, which would make her criminally responsible as well.

There was no questioning Ray's guilt in court. Investigators were able to prove that each of the five men had died at the other end of Ray's gun after being lured to work for the man and then used as pawns in a cattle fraud scheme. It was irrefutable evidence.

Ray was quickly found guilty on all five counts of murder and other related charges including fraud. He was sentenced to death by lethal injection. Even his own children celebrated Ray's death sentence, viewing it as justice served for the horrible way he treated everyone around him, and for the horrible acts he committed simply to make extra money without having to do extra work.

Throughout her trial, Faye continued to claim she had no involvement and no knowledge in Ray's actions—he had committed his crimes all by himself. Faye was simply an abused wife her put her head down and did what she was told to do. Throughout her life she had carried bruises and broken bones for nothing and had spent most of her life doing everything possible to avoid Ray's violence. Her greatest crime was not asking questions.

The list of workers in Faye Copeland's handwriting, however, sealed her fate. It was the smoking gun of the prosecutor's case, and it got Faye convicted for all five murders as well. She also received a sentence of death.

Before Ray Copeland could be executed he died in prison in 1993. Six years later, in 1999 Faye's attorneys appealed her conviction on the basis that Faye had been too terrified of her former husband to admit her life long abuse at his hands. The abuse had been the reason Faye had written the list, but jurors had never heard this before. The only previous explanation previously could have been that she was involved.

On this basis, the courts commuted her death sentence to life in prison, but her convictions remained. Three years later, Faye suffered a stroke which left her partially paralyzed and unable to speak. She was released from prison a week later on medical parole, fulfilling her final wish not to die in prison. Faye passed away from natural causes less than a year later on December 23, 2003.

BONUS:

Franklin Delano Floyd

Franklin Delano Floyd's life was a long series of strange and tragic occurrences, beginning with the death of his father when Floyd was just a year old. Floyd grew up in an orphanage and turned to a life of crime at a young age, earning himself a lengthy criminal record over his lifetime. By the age of 20, in the year 1963, he was imprisoned for the kidnapping and rape of a 4 year old girl. He escaped from prison, robbed a bank, and then served a ten year prison term.

Floyd was released on parole and soon after committed another crime, attempting to kidnap a woman. He was arrested but posted bail quickly. Floyd then disappeared, spending much of the rest of his life on the run from authorities and using false names to hide his true identity.

However, Floyd's string of disturbing and violent crimes didn't stop. Around the time he disappeared, in 1974, Floyd married a woman in North Carolina. Floyd kidnapped two of the woman's children, including her five year old daughter, Suzanne Sevakis, who came to be known as Sharon Marshall. Floyd raised Marshall as a daughter, though later evidence showed he molested her from a young age. The two moved frequently around the country and used aliases to conceal Floyd's identity.

In the late 1980's, Marshall graduated from high school. A few years later she gave birth to a son named Michael Hughes, who it was later determined was not Floyd's biological son. Soon after, Marshall began working as an exotic dancer. It was during this time, in April of 1989, that Floyd committed the murder of Cheryl Commesso, a fellow dancer at the club where Marshall worked.

Commesso's murder went unsolved for years. Later in 1989, Floyd and Marshall were married. But in 1990, Marshall was killed in a hit and run accident. The driver was never found, and Floyd remains the only suspect in the case to this day. Later that year, Floyd was arrested for the kidnapping he committed in 1973.

Floyd again served a short prison sentence and was released in 1993. But Floyd didn't stop his life of crime. Shortly after serving his time in prison, Floyd attacked another woman. He was arrested for this attack but released on bond. During this time, Floyd went to the elementary school of Michael Hughes, Marshall's son, who had been living with a foster family. He kidnapped Hughes and the school principal, leaving the principal tied to a tree in the woods. The principal was found and survived, but Hughes was never found.

Floyd was finally arrested again in 1994 for the kidnapping of Hughes, though this would be the last time he was incarcerated. In 1995, Commesso's remains were found. The same year, a truck that had belonged to Floyd was found to contain images of child pornography along with pictures of Commesso severely beaten. This evidence was used to convict Floyd of Commesso's murder. In 2002, Floyd was sentenced to death for the murder of Cheryl Commesso and the kidnapping of Michael Hughes.

Early Life

From a very young age, Franklin Delano Floyd led a troubled life. He was born on June 17, 1943 to Thomas H. Floyd and Della Jewel Floyd in the town of Barnsville, Georgia. He had four siblings—a brother Billy and three sisters, Dorothy, Shirley, and Tommye.

In June 1944, when Floyd was just one year old, his father passed away. This left Floyd and his four siblings in the care of his mother, an unstable woman who would go on to have several failed marriages and her own criminal record. In January of 1946, the young Floyd and his siblings were placed in the Georgia Baptist Children's Home by their mother. Floyd's sister Dorothy was later separated from the others and moved to another orphanage in Pinewood, Georgia.

Floyd's mother moved to Florida where she married and subsequently divorced twice. She then married her fourth husband, who she would stay with for the rest of her life. It is unlikely that Floyd ever saw his mother again, though she did visit his sister Dorothy once, a trip that ended with Della being arrested on a drunk and disorderly charge.

In the summer of 1959, when he turned sixteen, Floyd ran away from the children's home he had been living in since he was just two years old. Shortly after running away, Floyd obtained falsified documents claiming he was eighteen years old. He used these papers to join the U.S. Army, using his real name but a fake age.

Floyd's Army career was short-lived, however. He was stationed in Missouri and Oklahoma before his real age was discovered in December of 1959. Upon discovering he was only sixteen, the Army sent Floyd via bus to his sister Dorothy. Dorothy had married since leaving the orphanage and now lived in Gainesville, Georgia. When Floyd arrived, however, Dorothy's husband did not allow him to stay.

A few months later, Floyd began what would ultimately be a life of crime. Early in the morning on February 19, 1960, Floyd broke into a Sears store in Inglewood, California. Police arrived at the scene and Floyd exchanged fire with the police on the roof of the building. He was shot in the back and hospitalized for his injuries at Centinela Hospital.

After recovering somewhat, Floyd was transferred to the prison ward in nearby General Hospital before being sent to the Preston Youth Correctional Facility. His sentence was not long, and by the summer of 1961 Floyd was out on parole. However, in August of 1961 he violated his parole by leaving the country and going on a camping trip in Canada. Floyd was arrested in November of 1961 for this parole violation and was returned to the Preston Youth facility.

A few months later, in January of 1962, Floyd was released. He left California, returning to his home state of Georgia where he briefly lived with his sister Dorothy in Gainesville. He then moved nearer to Atlanta, where Floyd worked at the Atlanta airport for a short period of time. In May of 1962, Floyd moved back to Hapeville, Georgia and lived near the Georgia Baptist Children's Home where he grew up. It was during this time that Floyd, now nineteen years old, began to commit more horrific crimes.

Kidnapping and Bank Robbery

On May 20, 1962, Floyd kidnapped a four year old girl from a bowling alley in Hapeville, Georgia. Floyd subsequently raped the girl. On July 31, 1962 he was found guilty of child molestation and was sentenced to 20 years in prison. However, Floyd would never serve his full sentence for this crime.

Floyd was sent to Reidsville Prison in Atlanta, Georgia to serve his time. In November of 1962 he was hospitalized at Milledgeville Hospital where he underwent psychiatric testing. Floyd had a number of psychiatric problems, possibly stemming from his difficult childhood spent in an orphanage. His stay at the hospital was lengthy, spanning more than four months.

On March 14, 1963 Floyd escaped from Milledgeville Hospital. Outside the hospital, he stole a car and purchased a pellet pistol. Floyd used these to commit a bank robbery, later claiming he needed to get money to appeal his child molestation conviction. He stole over $6,800 from the Citizens and Southern Bank in Macon, Georgia, and was caught and arrested the same day. Floyd soon confessed to the crime.

On July 12, 1963, Floyd was sentenced to fifteen years in prison for the bank robbery. He was sent to Chillicothe Federal prison in Chillicothe, Ohio. Floyd remained there for several months, though in September of 1963 he attempted to escape by hotwiring a prison fire truck and crashing it into a fence. The escape attempt was unsuccessful.

In October, Floyd was transferred to a prison in Lewisburg, Pennsylvania where he remained until June of 1964, when he was sent to a prison hospital in Springfield, Missouri to be evaluated. Floyd stayed in the hospital for eight months before being transferred to a federal prison in Marion, Illinois.

The prison in Marion was Floyd's longest stay in one facility to that point, and he remained there from February of 1965 until February of 1968. During this time he earned his GED. Floyd's mother also passed away while he was in prison in Marion. In February 1968 Floyd was again transferred, this time back to Reidsville, Georgia. He finished his sentence for child molestation there.

In November 1971, Floyd was sent to a federal prison in Atlanta, Georgia to serve his sentence for his escape attempt in Chillicothe. He was there for another year, and in November 1972, Floyd was released to a halfway house. Soon after, on January 19, 1973 he was paroled.

Just over a week later, on January 27, 1973, Floyd attempted to kidnap a young woman. On February 2nd, he was arrested for the attack. Floyd called a friend he met during his time in prison who bailed him out. After this incident, Floyd disappeared for several years, becoming a fugitive on the run.

Sharon Marshall

Sometime between 1973 and 1975, Franklin Delano Floyd, using an alias, married a North Carolina woman by the name of Sandra Chipman. Chipman had four children, including a baby boy, a five year old girl, and two other daughters. In 1974, Chipman was arrested and served 30 days in jail for writing bad checks. While she was in jail, Floyd took two of her children—the baby boy and the five year old girl—and fled the state. The other two children were placed in a children's home.

When Chipman was released from jail, she was able to reunite with the two children Floyd had left behind. However, Floyd and her other two children were long gone. Chipman attempted to file a report with the police, but she was told that because Floyd was the children's stepfather he had the right to take them.

Chipman's infant son was never seen again, and his whereabouts remain unknown to this day. Her young daughter Suzanne Sevakis, however, remained with Floyd. He gave her several different aliases during her childhood, as he was still a fugitive, but as she grew older the girl went by the name of Sharon Marshall.

In 1975, Floyd got a job working for the Oklahoma school system. In August of 1975, he enrolled Marshall at Wilson Elementary School in Oklahoma. Floyd went by the false name of Trenton Davis while Marshall was enrolled in school as his daughter under the name Suzanne Davis.

In 1978, Floyd had to move again. A babysitter told police that she believed Floyd, or Trenton Davis, was molesting his "daughter". Floyd appeared again in Arizona briefly, where Marshall was again enrolled in school. They didn't stay long, moving to Louisville, Kentucky in 1979.

In 1983, Sharon Marshall began high school. She attended three different schools in 1983 as Floyd moved around, taking her with him. Floyd finally settled in Atlanta, Georgia, assuming the name Warren Marshall. Sharon Marshall enrolled in Forest Park High School, where she was a surprisingly successful student.

Marshall was a smart girl and a good student. By the time she graduated, she had even earned college scholarships for her academic excellence. Not just smart, Marshall was also a popular student. She ran for junior class office and, according to her teachers, was well-liked. She attended a student council leadership conference one summer, where she befriended Jennifer Tanner.

Tanner was later able to give accounts of her friendship with Marshall, shedding light onto Marshall's mysterious life. According to Tanner, Marshall's "father", Floyd, was very strict. She also stated later that Marshall showed her lingerie Floyd had given her. Adding to the strangeness of their relationship, Tanner also said that Floyd was obsessive about Marshall's looks, frequently taking photographs of the teenager.

In 1986, Sharon Marshall graduated high school. She had done well enough to earn a full scholarship to go to Georgia Tech and study aerospace engineering. However, she never went to college and instead stayed with Floyd. Marshall moved to Phoenix, Arizona with Floyd in July 1986. In 1988, Marshall got pregnant. She attempted to run away to Alabama to be with her boyfriend, but he woke up to find her missing one day. She left behind a note saying her father had taken her back with him. Marshall was back with Franklin Delano Floyd.

On March 21, 1988 Marshall gave birth to a baby boy and named him Michael Anthony Hughes. Even after Hughes's birth, Marshall and Floyd continued to move around frequently.

By April of 1989, Marshall and Floyd were living in Tampa, Florida. Marshall was working as an exotic dancer at the Mons Venus club. This is where they met Cheryl Commesso, the woman Floyd was ultimately sentenced to death for killing.

Cheryl Commesso

Cheryl Commesso was a native of the Tampa, Florida area. Just a few years younger than Marshall, she had attended the local Brandon High School, where she participated in extracurricular activities, including singing in the chorus and dancing. Commesso even competed in the Miss Brandon pageant in 1987. Commesso, according to surviving family members, was a bright young girl who just grew up too fast.

In her senior year of high school, Commesso began to run away. She dropped out of school and began dancing at the World Famous Doll House a strip club in Orlando, Florida. Commesso was living fast—she bought a red Corvette and earned enough money dancing to get breast implants. According to her mother, Lois Commesso, she wanted to model for Playboy someday.

In 1989, Commesso was working at the Mons Venus near Tampa, Florida, where she lived with her father. She met and befriended Sharon Marshall who was also working as a dancer at the club.

The friendship turned into a deadly mistake for Commesso. In late March of April 1989, shortly after St. Patrick's Day, Commesso and Marshall got into an argument outside the Mons Venus club. Floyd became involved, accusing Commesso of reporting Marshall for falsely reporting her income, which had resulted in Marshall losing Medicaid coverage for her infant son. According to a coworker of Commesso and Marshall's, Floyd punched Commesso during this argument, leaving a bruise.

Not long after the altercation, Commesso went missing. It was later discovered that Floyd, possibly with Marshall's help, had kidnapped Commesso. Nobody knows exactly where he took her or all the graphic details of what he did to her, but Floyd did leave some clues, whether he meant to or not.

Commesso was last seen by her family a few days before the murder. She was leaving for several days. Commesso packed a bag and told her father she would call him soon, then left, never to be seen alive again. Her car was soon found in the parking lot of the St. Petersburg/ Clearwater airport. This immediately aroused suspicions in her family, who told police that Commesso was very attached to her car and would never have left it.

Commesso's fate remained unknown for years. Finally, in 1995, landscapers found her skeletal remains in a wooded area off of Interstate 275. Medical investigators determined the woman whose skeleton they found, known at the time as "Jane Doe I-25", had been beaten and shot in the back of the head twice. They were also able to identify the body as Commesso's, with evidence suggesting the body had been there for six to seven years, the same amount of time as Commesso had been missing.

Back on the Run

Floyd's other criminal enterprises did not stop during this time. In April of 1989, the very same month that Commesso was murdered, a warrant was placed on Floyd for insurance fraud. Floyd was accused of drilling holes into the bottom of a boat he owned in order to collect insurance money.

Floyd and Marshall were also the primary suspects in Commesso's mysterious disappearance, thanks to the altercation coworkers had witnessed between Floyd and Commesso shortly before she disappeared. Floyd left town soon after murdering Commesso and brought Marshall along with him. The pair left Tampa, Florida in May of 1989 and moved to New Orleans. On June 15, 1989, Floyd and Marshall married, with both the bride and groom using new aliases.

The very next day, June 16, 1989, Floyd's trailer in Tampa burned to the ground. Police ruled that this was intentional arson. Most likely, Floyd was attempting to hide the evidence of Commesso's murder as well as his own identity, as he was still wanted for the 1973 kidnapping case in Atlanta. It appeared that, at least for the moment, Floyd was going to keep running from the law.

Soon after these events, Floyd and Marshall moved again, this time to Tulsa, Oklahoma. In August of 1989, Marshall began working at another adult entertainment nightclub called Passion. She and Floyd would live together in Oklahoma for several months with Marshall working as a dancer. Coworkers say that Marshall was secretive about her past, telling them only that all members of her family were dead.

During her time at Passions, Marshall also confided in some of her coworkers, though she never revealed the truth about her life. She did, however, tell coworkers that she had a new boyfriend whom she had met at the club. Marshall's coworkers claim she was afraid to tell her husband that she wanted to leave him.

Marshall was right to fear what Floyd might do. Less than a year after their marriage in New Orleans, Marshall was killed in a mysterious hit-and-run accident.

Hit-and-Run

On the night of April 25, 1990, the woman who had come to be known as Sharon Marshall was struck by a car while walking on the side of the road to the motel where she was staying in Tulsa. Marshall was hospitalized and survived for five days with her injuries before dying on

April 30, 1990. Her funeral was held in Tulsa, Oklahoma on May 4, 1990.

Floyd was a person of interest in the case. He claimed that he was in the motel waiting for her and therefore could not have been the driver in the hit-and-run accident. Floyd was not arrested, though police had their suspicions.

On May 17, 1990, less than two weeks after his mother's death Michael Hughes, Marshall's son, was declared a ward of the state. Hughes was placed in foster care. According to his foster parents, Hughes, who was two years old, was non-verbal and had limited muscle control. His behavior was frequently out of control. Nevertheless, Hughes began to make progress during his time with his foster family.

Identity Revealed

On June 20, 1990, Floyd was finally caught and his true identity as Franklin Delano Floyd was revealed. He was arrested near Augusta, Georgia where he had been living in a trailer, for the 1973 kidnapping attempt he had committed in Atlanta. Floyd was sent to a federal prison in Georgia, and in December of 1990 he was transferred to El Reno Prison in Oklahoma.

Floyd spent a total of 33 months in El Reno Prison. During this time, Michael Hughes's foster parents began the process of adopting Hughes. As part of this process, Hughes's DNA was compared to Floyd's to establish paternity. It was discovered that Floyd was not Hughes's biological father, a fact that would later keep him from gaining custody of Hughes.

On March 30, 1993, Floyd was released to a halfway house. He began working as a maintenance man at an apartment complex. Not long after, he returned to his old ways. On July 4, 1994, Floyd attacked a woman at the apartment complex where he worked. Floyd hid in the bushes of the apartment complex and attempted to attack the woman with a knife when she came home. He was arrested for the attack on August 19, 1994 and was released on bond that same day.

Kidnapping

After he was released from prison, Floyd tried to regain custody of Michael Hughes. However, due to his lengthy criminal record and the recent finding that he had no biological relation to Hughes, a judge denied Floyd's request.

Floyd took matters into his own hands. On September 12, 1994, Floyd went to the elementary school in Choctaw, Oklahoma, where Hughes was in the first grade. Floyd entered the office of Principal James Davis and demanded to see his son. He told Davis he had a gun and showed the gun to Davis, telling him, "If you don't help me, you won't live."

Davis took Floyd to Hughes, and Floyd drove all three of them into the woods in Davis's pickup truck. There, Floyd handcuffed Davis to a tree and left with Hughes.

It's not clear what happened to Hughes after this. Floyd would claim later that Hughes was safe somewhere, then later changed his story and began to say he had killed Hughes.

Floyd returned to Georgia, committing a carjacking in Atlanta. He was also a patient at Grady Memorial Hospital in Atlanta, Georgia from September 21-29, 1994. Floyd didn't stay long, and in October of 1994 Principal Davis's truck was found near the Love Field Airport in Dallas, Texas, suggesting Floyd had been in the area.

Floyd was ultimately apprehended in Louisville, Kentucky. He was arrested on November 10, 1994 at a Kentucky car dealership where he had just started working two days prior. The arrest was for the kidnapping charge, but Floyd would soon be implicated in the murder of Cheryl Commesso.

Putting the Pieces Together

In March of 1995, Cheryl Commesso's body was finally found on the side of I-275 in Tampa, Florida. Meanwhile, the truck that Floyd had stolen when he kidnapped Davis was sold, and the new owner made a disturbing discovery. A thick envelope stuffed with dozens of pictures was found wedged between the bed of the truck and the gas tank.

Some of the pictures showed Cheryl Commesso being tortured and beaten. Others were photographs of Sharon Marshall dating back to when she was a young girl, showing her in sexually suggestive poses. The pictures of Commesso showed her wearing the same jewelry that was found on her body, and there were also pictures of the inside of a trailer and other items that belonged to Floyd. Finally, one picture showed part of someone's thumb. Investigators were able to match the thumb to Floyd. This, along with the photographs of Marshall and Floyd's belongings, was enough evidence to charge Floyd with murder.

On September 28, 2002, Floyd was convicted of first degree murder. The trial had lasted only 90 days and jurors deliberated for just four hours before reaching a guilty verdict. Floyd had an outburst in the courtroom, claiming the prosecutors had framed him and swearing at the judge.

On November 22, 2002, Floyd was sentenced to death. Judge Nancy Moate Ley read the verdict, acknowledging that Floyd had had a difficult childhood, but his long criminal record and the particularly horrific nature of his crime made it necessary for him to be sentenced to death. It was, according to Ley, "not surprising" that the jury had decided on the death penalty.

Floyd is currently on death row in Union Correctional Institution awaiting execution. Many mysteries still surround Franklin Delano Floyd and the crimes he committed. No one has yet been arrested in the hit-and-run accident that killed Sharon Marshall.

In 2014, DNA evidence was used to discover the true identity of Sharon Marshall, linking her to Sandra Chipman. Finally, the truth about Suzanne Sevakis, the North Carolina girl who had been missing for decades, and Sharon Marshall, the mystery girl Floyd had kidnapped, was revealed—they were the same person.

Floyd would also later confess to murdering Michael Hughes, though there is no proof of this claim and no remains have been found. Floyd was able to identify a location in the woods where he claims he killed Hughes. The truth, however, like so many things about Franklin Delano Floyd, may never be known.